100
GREAT
PR
IDEAS

FROM LEADING COMPANIES
AROUND THE WORLD

Jim Blythe

Marshall Cavendish
Business

Copyright © 2009 Jim Blythe

First published in 2009 by

Marshall Cavendish Editions
An imprint of Marshall Cavendish International
1 New Industrial Road, Singapore 536196

Other Marshall Cavendish offices: Marshall Cavendish Ltd. 5th Floor, 32–38 Saffron Hill, London RC1N 8FH, UK • Marshall Cavendish Corporation. 99 White Plains Road, Tarrytown NY 10591-9001, USA • Marshall Cavendish International (Thailand) Co Ltd. 253 Asoke, 12th Flr, Sukhumvit 21 Road, Klongtoey Nua, Wattana, Bangkok 10110, Thailand • Marshall Cavendish (Malaysia) Sdn Bhd, Times Subang, Lot 46, Subang Hi-Tech Industrial Park, Batu Tiga, 40000 Shah Alam, Selangor Darul Ehsan, Malaysia

Marshall Cavendish is a trademark of Times Publishing Limited

A CIP record for this book is available from the British Library

ISBN 978-0-462-09949-1

Designed by Robert Jones
Project managed by Cambridge Publishing Management Ltd

Printed in Singapore by Fabulous Printers Pte Ltd

CONTENTS

INTRODUCTION

PR, OR PUBLIC relations, has been variously defined. For some people, the letters PR stand for "press release," because this is such a common way for PR people to get the message out there. In fact, though, PR is about creating good relationships with the organization's publics. Those publics include customers, suppliers, government departments, pressure groups such as Greenpeace or Friends of the Earth, other businesses who are our neighbors, or indeed anybody who is, or might be, affected by what we do.

Public relations is a lot more than kissing people all over. It's a long-term activity: what we are trying to do is to create a good image of ourselves, but more importantly an accurate image of ourselves, in people's minds. We don't necessarily do everything we can to please people, either: sometimes we have to agree to differ, and simply show ourselves to be fair-minded.

Public relations people always have to work through others: through the news media, through other organizations, through the staff of the firms they work for. There is therefore a premium on good social skills, but this doesn't mean being a backslapping, joke-telling pain in the neck. It means considering the needs (and agendas) of other people, whether it is the journalist who needs a good story to fill a space in this evening's paper, or an environmental activist who wants to prove that he has made us change our policy on recycling. In other words, good PR people are able to empathize with other people, even with enemies—this is an important quality.

The ideas in this book have come from many sources. Some have come directly from the firms themselves, some have come from PR professionals, some have come from the news media that are the lifeblood of public relations. At this point I should make special mention of Joan Stewart of The Publicity Hound (www. PublicityHound.com), who generously gave me a large number of basic ideas that I adapted for Britain. All of them are tried and tested, but you should be wary of simply copying something slavishly—often the ideas have worked simply because they are very newsworthy, and the point about news is that it is something that hasn't happened before.

This means that PR is not a formulaic activity. It requires creativity, originality, and the ability to take a risk in order to create something that has impact. Some PR is "slow burn": some of the ideas in the book would take years or even decades to have a real impact. Some ideas are quick fixes—they provide an instant burst of publicity, or a rapid response to an event. PR people need to be able to cope with both types of activity—the rapid response and the gradual build— and probably need to be running both types of activity at once.

This book is aimed at a fairly broad audience. If you have no experience of PR, it offers some ideas to get you off the starting blocks: if you are an experienced PR professional, I hope it will offer you a few ideas you haven't thought of yet. Some of the ideas work best for small firms, some for larger firms: some work best for non-profit organizations, some for commercial organizations. Some are most effective in service industries, others work best for manufacturing or retailing.

Whatever your reason for picking up this book, you will undoubtedly get some thoughts provoked—after all, that's what PR is all about!

Jim Blythe

1 CREATE A CRISIS TEAM

BAD THINGS HAPPEN in most industries from time to time. Some industries are especially prone to newsworthy incidents—airlines are an obvious example—while others may go for years without anything happening that would hit the headlines. However, if a crisis does occur, it is amazing how fast it can turn from a simple, solvable problem into a PR disaster.

For many firms, such a crisis can be enough to destroy the company. When a Pan American Airlines flight was destroyed by terrorists over Lockerbie, the company suffered a PR disaster when it emerged that warnings had been given about a bomb on the aircraft. The fact that PanAm received an average of four bomb warnings a day made no difference to the public perception: shortly afterward, PanAm went out of business.

The problem was that PanAm did not have an effective crisis management protocol.

The idea

Many companies have a well-established crisis team who anticipate scenarios that may create PR problems, and work out solutions in advance. When Eurolines, the European long-distance bus company, suffered a crisis, they had a plan in place. A Eurolines bus from Warsaw to London was hit by a lorry in Germany, injuring a number of passengers (some seriously). The company's crisis team were ready: some passengers were hospitalized in Germany, some were given the option of returning to Warsaw, others were given the option of continuing to London.

At the London end, a large hotel was booked to receive passengers. Medical staff were on hand to provide help (although of course all injured passengers had already received medical care in Germany) and interpreters were available. The passenger list was checked to determine the nationalities of passengers—not all were Poles, since some had traveled to Warsaw from Lithuania, Latvia, Estonia, and even Russia to meet the connection in Poland. Rooms were booked for all passengers and also for friends or family who had expected to meet the coach. Eurolines' operations director was also present, as well as the PR officer, to field questions from the press and specifically to prevent reporters from harassing passengers for comments. A buffet was provided for all those present, and the following day Eurolines issued free tickets for onward connections in Britain, recognizing that many passengers would have missed their connections or whoever was meeting them in London.

The organization was exemplary: efficient, effective, and geared to creating goodwill all around. Such a slick approach does not happen by accident—it only happens through careful planning and rehearsal.

In practice

- Choose the right people to be on the team. They need to be senior enough to carry credibility with the firm's publics, and to understand the possible problems and solutions.

- Arrange for the crisis team to meet regularly to consider possible scenarios.

- Practice—do dummy runs.

- Ensure that team members know how to deal with the press—having someone say "No comment" to every question is a PR disaster in itself.

2 DEFINE YOUR OPPONENT

Knowing your opponent is one thing—defining them in the minds of your publics is another. Most PR exercises are about defining the organization in the minds of its publics, but this is only half the story, especially when one is confronted with a persistent opponent who cannot be placated.

The problem is made worse by the fact that people often identify with the underdog, which means that direct attacks on opponents are very likely to backfire. Subtlety is needed! The way forward for many organizations is to use wording that conveys a solidly positive image, forcing opponents to take up the negative stance.

The idea

By categorizing yourself in a positive way it is easy to imply that your opponents are categorized in a negative way. The topic of abortion is an extremely emotive one, for example: those in favor of it categorize themselves as "pro-choice," which means that any opponents immediately categorize themselves as "anti-choice." Those same opponents categorize themselves as "pro-life," which tends to make opponents categorize themselves as "anti-life" in the public consciousness.

For firms in less emotive industries, there is the possibility of categorizing the firm as "pro-jobs" or "on the side of economic growth in the region." This immediately wrong-foots opponents, who then need to justify their own positions.

Forcing opponents into a negative position provides you with an immediate advantage in establishing your own credibility in the minds of your publics. Unless your opponents are very slick, you will have gained the high ground.

In practice

- Find the positives.

- Choose the positive that forces your opponents into a negative position.

- Do not muddy the waters—keep plugging the positive term you have decided on.

- Be prepared for retaliation. Your opponents will probably respond in kind.

DO GOOD BY STEALTH

MANY FIRMS MAKE a big song-and-dance about their charity work, promoting their generosity in sponsoring this or that good cause. This is all well and good, but can easily backfire: a firm that continually harps on about its good corporate citizenship makes people wonder whether it is only contributing to charity in order to look good—in the same way as a rich person suddenly becomes overwhelmingly generous as death approaches, the suspicion is that the firm (like the person) is simply trying to buy its way into heaven.

The alternative is to keep fairly quiet about charitable behavior—but how can this benefit the company?

The idea

Body Shop is world renowned for its unusual approach to the cosmetics business, and indeed to business in general. Founder Anita Roddick famously said that she didn't believe in marketing, but in fact she was eminently good at doing it: she was equally good at public relations, and elevated Body Shop in many ways.

One of the most important aspects of the Body Shop organization is that each store is encouraged to carry out charity work within the local community. Staff can choose which projects they want to become involved in, and can decide their own way of contributing, with the support of the firm.

This means that local Body Shop branches might be involved in creating a children's playgroup, in supporting a local hospice, in fundraising for a kidney machine for the local hospital, or in any one of hundreds of different ways. Staff sometimes volunteer their time to help, sometimes collect money, sometimes lobby local councils to act. Body Shop allows them time off work to do this, but many staff members carry on in their own time as well.

The result of this approach is that staff feel part of the local community, they feel that they are working for an ethical employer, and they feel more like part of a team. In the local area, word soon gets around that Body Shop is helping: the publicity arises through word of mouth, rather than as the result of press releases or advertising. This is surely the most powerful way of generating interest.

In practice

- Involve your staff—in fact for preference put them in charge of the project.

- Support your staff effort. If you can't give them time off, let them use company facilities or provide them with funding—perhaps by matching any money they raise.

- Do not be tempted to publicize what they are doing. This is likely to damage the word-of-mouth effect and dilute the impact of the exercise.

- Accept that results may be a long time in coming, and there will be problems along the way as staff make errors or choose inappropriate projects. Don't be afraid to let them learn.

4 PULL A STUNT

THE HISTORY OF public relations is littered with publicity stunts. The aim of a stunt is to generate word of mouth—a good stunt can keep people talking for days. The best stunts are ones that relate to the product and that are eye-catching and creative—good street theater, in other words.

Stunts also need to appeal to the target audience, of course. Some stunts might be regarded as offensive or unacceptable—and some even border on the illegal, as happened with one drinks company that engaged graffiti artists to spray the company logo onto buildings in London. Finding a suitable stunt is a matter of balancing good taste with powerful impact. One company found a startling way to do this.

The idea

One classic stunt was the fight staged between a well-known bandleader and a bystander, allegedly over the recipe for Pimm's. The PR man who organized the stunt paid both men to stage a street brawl, with the press on hand: naturally, the stunt made the headlines, and generated a great deal of word of mouth at relatively little cost.

Staging a fight between a celebrity and a bystander works fine if the celebrity agrees that such behavior accords with his or her public image. For the target audience, this event was both shocking and fascinating, and also enhanced the image of the product by making it seem worth fighting for.

It actually doesn't matter a great deal if it later becomes public knowledge that the stunt was staged—people are quite used to the concept of the spoof!

In practice

- Ensure that your stunt is legal.

- Remember that the stunt must fit in with the images of the people involved.

- Be wary of upsetting the journalists—they do not like being fooled, any more than do the rest of us, but they are usually happy to go along with a spoof.

SET AN AMBUSH

AMBUSH PR IS about riding on the back of someone else's expenditure, and it happens frequently when companies sponsor events. Although being an official sponsor of a major event such as the football World Cup or the Wimbledon tennis tournament carries a great deal of publicity value, it does cost a lot of money as well, and often the sponsors are lost among a welter of other organizations so that the payoff becomes hard to identify.

The idea

During the 1998 soccer World Cup, held in France, Nike and adidas were clear rivals. The major advantage of soccer from a PR viewpoint is its ability to attract world TV audiences, so for global brands such as Nike and adidas the attraction is obvious.

The organizers of the World Cup, FIFA, only allow one main sponsor in each business category, so Nike and adidas could not both sponsor the event. adidas "won the toss" and became the official sponsor, even though some of the competing teams were sponsored by Nike: the sponsorship fee was reputed to be £20 million, but Nike was able to ambush the event for a great deal less.

Nike set up a "football village" among the startling buildings at La Défense, on the northern edge of Paris. Entry was free, and the company laid on a number of "fun" events aimed at young soccer fans. Nike was not allowed to use the World Cup logo, or even refer to the event directly, but most people visiting the Nike village were blissfully unaware of this. The company even set up a "road show" to tour France, giving schoolchildren the chance to play against a

Nigerian under-17 international team. Nike's expenditure on the village was only £4.2 million, much less than adidas's investment, for very similar results.

Ambushing adidas's efforts not only gave Nike an unearned advantage: it also detracted from the impact of adidas's PR exercise. adidas were not quick enough off the mark in countering Nike, but it is hard to see what they might have done to prevent Nike's actions.

In practice

- Find an event that links to your product in a fairly direct way.

- Carry out your own activities in as close a proximity to the main event as you are able.

- Do not make any direct statements linking your firm to the event—let your actions speak for themselves.

- Expect retaliation.

6 BE HUMOROUS

HUMOR HAS ALWAYS been a good way to get people to feel positive about the organization. Many companies produce humorous advertisements, but there is no reason why PR should not also operate with a sense of fun.

Sponsorship has always been a popular tool of PR: it generates word of mouth and creates a good impression of the firm. Some firms have even managed to make sponsorship fun by backing something humorous.

The idea

Hamlet cigars have always taken a humorous approach to their promotion. The adverts were so well liked that they were released on video—no small achievement in the advertising world. When tobacco advertising was banned throughout Europe, most tobacco companies scrambled to sponsor sporting events, arts events, and indeed anything that was not advertising. The brand managers for Hamlet decided to continue with their humorous approach, and sought out something jokey to sponsor.

Thus was born the Bad Sex Award. Hamlet sponsored a prize by the *Literary Review* for the most badly written sex scenes in new literature. The 2004 award went to famous American author Tom Wolfe, who is reputed to be the only author who did not turn up to claim his prize.

Sponsorship has now also been banned for tobacco companies, which has left a void in the funding of many organizations:

however, for a time the Bad Sex Award offered Hamlet a great way to promote itself.

In practice

- Look for something that your target audience likes.

- Tap into their sense of humor: this may or may not be the same as your own.

- Help the people you sponsor to publicize themselves.

7 KEEP THEM WAITING

MOST PR PEOPLE like to blow the fanfare when they have something new to promote. After all, it is a great opportunity to show what can be done with an effective PR campaign, and enables them to give the media something really meaty for a change.

Yet it is a truism in PR that the greatest successes come from doing something different from what everyone else is doing. So why not have a non-launch, and keep people waiting for the product?

The idea

The Harry Potter books have been a huge success, making their author, J. K. Rowling, a multimillionaire. New Harry Potter books were big news, and the publishers were good at teasing the readers: when *Harry Potter and the Goblet of Fire* was published in 2000, bookstores were prevented from selling the book (although they were allowed to display copies in locked cages). News reports came in that 20 copies had accidentally been sold by a nameless supermarket: TV footage of the books being delivered to bookstores in security vans was shown, and (mysteriously) a copy of the book found its way onto the news desk of the *Scottish Daily Record*, upon which the journalists (equally mysteriously) returned it to the publishers unopened.

Eventually the official launch took place on July 8th, 2000. Needless to say, there were queues around the block to buy the book.

In practice

- Ensure that you have something that people will find exciting anyway: this idea works best for new products in a series, such as new models of car, book and movie sequels, and new menu items in restaurants.

- Set a date for the release of the product and publicize it.

- Limit the number of outlets or the supply of products—this is more likely to create an initial frenzy.

HOLD A COMPETITION

COMPETITIONS, LOTTERIES, CONTESTS of any sort always attract attention, but some are more newsworthy than others. Competitors remember the firm, and often talk about the competition, but the best outcome is, of course, if the competition makes the news in some way.

Some types of competition are better than others for this.

The idea

In 1958, the mayor's office in a small Spanish fishing village made a major strategic decision. They decided that the village should try to attract more foreign tourists. The village itself was picturesque, it was near to a new international airport, and package holidays by air were just beginning to become available. The mayor envisaged a town with a few small hotels, attracting well-off northern Europeans to inject some cash into the local economy, which was suffering greatly under Franco's dictatorship.

The mayor's office decided to organize a song contest. Songwriters and performers were invited to the village, and a series of performances were organized: the song contest was intended to be newsworthy, and to attract the kind of middle-class audience the village was trying to cultivate. A recording deal was on offer for the winner (and of course recording studios were very happy to sign up any promising losers as well).

In the event, the winning song became a major hit, not only in Spain but throughout the Spanish-speaking world. The village itself gained dramatically from the publicity, and although the mayor's original concept for the village disappeared, it disappeared under a colossal injection of investment: the original fishing village was overwhelmed by the mass of concrete hotels that now characterize the town it has become—it is, of course, Benidorm.

Whatever we might think of Benidorm, it is certainly a prosperous place and a lot of money has been made: and it all started with a song contest.

In practice

- Choose a competition topic that is newsworthy.

- Invite specific contestants if at all possible—if not, ensure that your pre-publicity is targeted at contestants who will generate publicity themselves.

- Ensure that the competition is strongly branded.

WRITE A REVERSE PYRAMID

PRESS RELEASES ARE the mainstay of public relations, yet many firms do not handle them well. Many press releases are simply thinly disguised advertisements, and of course periodicals will not print these for free: they expect to get paid for running advertisements.

Press releases have the big advantage that periodicals do publish them for free. They also have an even bigger advantage—people read them, even when they have skipped past the advertisements.

The key to getting a press release published is to make it as easy as possible for the journalists and editors to use the release as it stands, without having to rewrite it. Newspapers have a lot of space to fill, every day of the week, and going out to research news stories is both time-consuming and expensive. Like any of us, journalists are more than happy to save time and effort—so a well-written press release can be a godsend on a day when news is slack and the paper needs to be filled.

The idea

A press release is a news story about your company. The point here is it should be news—something that is out of the ordinary, and that will be interesting to the newspaper's readers. A story about your latest sales promotion is not interesting unless there is something very unusual about the promotion, but a story about your new factory creating 250 new jobs in a depressed area is interesting.

The story needs to be written in a way that journalists and editors relate to. Journalists are trained to write in a "reverse pyramid" style.

The whole story is contained in the headline, then each paragraph offers a little more detail: the intention is that the story can be cut from the bottom by a subeditor to fit the available space. The best way to get the idea of how to do this is to read some newspaper stories: it is easy to see how the story is complete at each paragraph.

Press releases should also be written for the specific periodical. A story about a breakthrough in engineering techniques might be interesting to an engineering trade journal, but would not be interesting to *Cosmopolitan*: an article about your new female chief engineer would have the reverse characteristics.

In practice

- Write in the style of the journal you are aiming for.

- The press release must be news—not just a thinly disguised advertisement.

- Make things easy for the journalists by writing in a reverse pyramid style.

- Cultivate your local newspaper—get friendly with the journalist who is most likely to be interested in what you have to say, then when you have a story it will be more likely to be used.

10 RUN A MEDIA EVENT

HOLDING A MEDIA event (sometimes called a press conference) is a great thing to do if you have something important to announce, but many firms only do it when there is a crisis. Obviously, anything you do announce needs to be real news—otherwise the journalists will, like anyone else, be annoyed at the waste of time involved.

Media events give the journalists a chance to ask questions in a way that a press release does not. It enables them to build a story around their own needs—or the needs of their particular publication—and to investigate areas that the company may or may not want to have brought to light.

Handling a media event properly isn't always straightforward, but the payoffs are potentially huge.

The idea

A media event should only be called when there is something that the journalists will find interesting. The event should be publicized as far in advance as possible, and you should ensure that it is held at a time that will not cause problems for journalists who are on deadlines—for example, newspapers have strict deadlines, and they are unlikely to stop the presses unless you are announcing World War III.

Refreshments should be laid on, but you should not be too lavish—reporters can be suspicious that they are being softened up with an expensive buffet. Senior management must be present to field questions, and they must also be briefed on how to handle questions.

Far too many executives regard the press as a nuisance, and answer "no comment" to anything they are asked.

You should try to build in some time for journalists to talk one-on-one with the movers and shakers in your organization. Understandably, journalists prefer to have an angle that other journalists don't have, so announcing everything to everybody does not go down well.

It is worth while to contact local journalists on a regular basis with news or offers to provide advice and comments on news events—this will make them more inclined to attend media events in future.

In practice

- Time the event to suit the journalists' deadlines.

- Consult your local journalists beforehand.

- Ensure that senior managers are on hand, and that they are well briefed on the types of question to be asked and the appropriate replies.

- Remember that the media are on your side as long as they can see some benefit for themselves.

11 CATCH THEM YOUNG

Most PR ACTIVITIES are aimed at adult publics—government departments, customers, employees, the general public, and so on. Yet we know that people start forming their opinions of companies long before they are in a position to do business with them. Even children form clear brand associations at a very early age, so why not try to get to them before the competition does?

Of course, finding a suitable vehicle for doing so is the problem. Children are not big media consumers (apart from television) and are unlikely to read a press release.

The idea

Many companies sponsor sports teams: in fact as a PR exercise sports teams and sports events are probably the commonest forms of sponsorship. Children obviously see this type of sponsorship, and are certainly not immune to it: but how about sponsoring something the children themselves see as something for themselves?

Roy of the Rovers was the hero of a soccer magazine from 1954 to 2000. His fictional team, Melchester Rovers, had several sponsors, including McDonald's, TSB, Subbuteo, and Nike. Sponsoring a fictional football team may seem like a bizarre idea, but there are many advantages. First, it's a way of reaching a very young audience. Second, it's fairly certain that the team will win each week, will not become involved in drug scandals, and will remain reasonably sober and well behaved at away fixtures. Third, the comics are frequently kept and reread, often many times over. Fourth, the sponsorship adds credibility to the comic strip, which helps the credibility of the sponsor as well. Finally, it is usually a great deal cheaper to sponsor a fictional team than it is to sponsor a real one—no small consideration.

As time goes on, and comics become replaced by computer games, other sponsorship deals are likely to arise. It is obviously important to keep up with the times.

In practice

- Try to choose something that adds to the authenticity of both the sponsored "team" and the company.

- Keep in regular contact with the artists and writers who work on your "team."

- Generate ideas for storylines involving your brand.

PRESS YOUR JOURNALIST

MOST JOURNALISTS WORK long and often unsocial hours, and are not especially well paid. As a profession, they are often vilified and rarely praised except by their fellow journalists: today's news is wrapping tomorrow's fish, so journalists are constantly under pressure to perform.

Also, journalists do not exist in order to promote corporate products and reputations. Most of them are professional about what they do, and will only publish stories that are accurate, fair, and (above all) newsworthy.

The idea

Tyler Barnett, the owner of the Barnett Ellman PR agency in Los Angeles, sent a compliment to a magazine editor. "Journalists want to know their work is being read by someone, somewhere," he said. "We are all working hard, and can always use a nice compliment to brighten the day."

Make sure you read the journals, magazines, or newspapers you are hoping to place stories in. If your journalist has written a piece that you like, simply email him or her to say so. You don't necessarily need to do this every time, and especially you should not do it only when you want something, but an occasional word of praise will make your path a lot easier when you have something to report.

There is no need to be excessively effusive, either—find something in the article that you genuinely liked, and say so. The chances are other people liked it too, and also the writer himself (or herself) might well have felt proud of it even before your kind comments arrived.

In practice

- Don't be too effusive—it will sound false if you gush all over the place.

- Only give praise when it's deserved, and congratulations when they've been earned.

- Only do this with a journalist with whom you already have a relationship.

13 THINK SMALL

MAJOR MEDIA SUCH as national newspapers and TV news are notoriously difficult to get into. Apart from anything else, they are often bombarded with press releases, most of which are of limited interest. Local media such as local radio news, local TV news, and local newspapers are much easier to approach.

In business-to-business markets the smaller trade journals are also easier to get into, since they are likely to be more specialized and have fewer news-gathering resources.

The idea

Jason Calacanis, founder of *Silicon Alley Reporter* (a small specialist magazine for internet enthusiasts), found that major media outlets were not usually interested in him or his company. He recommends working through small media outlets rather than pitching to the big boys.

Pitching a press release at a smaller medium is usually easier and more likely to succeed. They have more time for you, and in any case the bigger media regularly trawl through the minor magazines looking for stories. This means that your story could well make it into the majors anyway.

Additionally, a small local paper or magazine exists to disseminate local news and human-interest stories, so they are much more likely to accept your piece. They have fewer resources for news gathering, and fewer press releases coming in.

Calacanis also recommends going to blog sites and contributing: either you can send the web link to the media you want to contact, or (fairly probably) they will find it themselves.

In practice

- Choose your media carefully.

- Remember that your press release might be picked up by bigger media, and be prepared to respond as necessary.

- Small specialist magazines rely on contacts with industry, so be prepared to answer questions.

KNOW YOUR JOURNALIST

JOURNALISTS ARE ALWAYS getting poorly targeted and poorly written press releases. This is an annoying waste of time—the working equivalent of junk mail—and certainly does not improve their perception of PR people.

It's easy to forget that journalists are human beings. They have names that need to be pronounced correctly, they have specific areas of interest within their jobs and outside work, and they resent time-wasters as much as any of us do.

The idea

Get hold of copies of the journalist's last five stories and read them. Make notes as you go. This is unlikely to take more than five minutes per story, but it will give you a good understanding of the individual you are dealing with.

From your reading, you will know the type of stories the journalist is interested in, and the style of his or her writing, and you will have a set of conversational topics for any meetings with the person. All of this will make it much more likely that information about your organization will be published, and is in any case no more than polite behavior.

Having this kind of knowledge shows that you are taking an interest in the journalist and the periodical, and enables you to create something that will be of real interest to its readers. This dramatically increases the chances of its being published.

In practice

- Be prepared to spend some time and effort investigating your target journalist.

- Get your facts straight before you call or contact the person.

- Remember that poorly targeted or poorly written press releases only irritate the journalists.

15 ● BE CONTROVERSIAL

Breaking through information clutter is a perennial problem. Many corporate communicators (marketers or PR people) try to cut through by being louder or more prolific than other people, while others try to be more fascinating than anyone else.

With audiences being exposed to literally thousands of messages per day, it is no surprise that most people quickly learn to filter out unwanted messages. If we were not able to do this, we would quickly suffer from information overload. This does, of course, leave corporate communicators with a problem.

The idea

Starbucks is the world's largest coffee shop chain, yet it uses virtually no advertising. The company is frequently in the news, however, and recently managed to create a controversial story simply by changing its logo.

Starbucks is represented by a mermaid with a forked tail. The mermaid appears on the front of the stores, on the cups, on the letterheads, on the staff's aprons, and indeed everywhere in the coffee shops themselves. Since the company was founded, the logo has changed several times, but the most recent version caused a furore because the mermaid now reveals rather more of her breasts than was the case on previous logos.

This new logo provoked the wrath of the born-again Christians in America: San Diego religious group The Resistance mounted a campaign to have the logo changed or withdrawn, despite the fact that the original Starbucks (dating back to the first coffee shops in San Francisco) actually showed the mermaid's nipples.

Although it may seem a little odd that people get so worked up about a cartoon mermaid's breasts, there is no doubt that the controversy has helped keep Starbucks in the public eye, and the fact that the objectors are who they are has probably been a positive for the brand.

In practice

- Be careful not to go so far as to offend your publics.

- Ensure that news of your controversial actions reaches the ears of people who will prove to be useful enemies.

- Try not to do anything irreversible—if the actions overstep the line, you may need to retract.

BE PROMINENT ON GOOGLE

THE INTERNET HAS, of course, wrought many changes in the way businesses operate. One of the major ones is in corporate communications, simply because people no longer sit around waiting for companies to communicate with them. Typically, people seek out information online, and in fact control the flow of information.

This has major implications for public relations. People seek out information from sources that they find agreeable, either from the viewpoint of being familiar and easy to use or from the viewpoint of having content that matches with the individual's own views. People are not passive recipients of information, and the internet allows them to take this further by choosing which company's websites they go to.

The idea

Ensuring that your website comes up in the first ten search results is the aim. This is because few people go beyond the first page of their Google search, and most only look at the first one or two pages. Choosing the right keywords when setting up your site is crucial, as is ensuring that the site content contains words that people are likely to use when searching the internet.

In larger firms, media relations tends to be relegated to the "nice to have if only we could afford it" list. Having an effective web presence is an important way to maintain a high PR profile at little or no cost.

In practice

- Choose your keywords carefully, based on what your publics are likely to enter into their search engines.

- Ensure that your content will not disappoint.

- Visit the website regularly yourself and encourage others to do so—this tends to move it up the list in terms of search results.

17 BE THE BRAND

In most businesses, people tend to separate their home and working lives. A lot of people who are running their own businesses tend to do likewise, switching off from business at the end of the day. A reluctance to talk about work is typical of many British entrepreneurs, and yet somebody who is committed and enthusiastic about what he or she does for a living is always interesting to talk to.

For good PR experts the day never ends: truly successful people are always prepared to talk about what they do. Many successful entrepreneurs are asked to talk to assemblies of people—sometimes at short notice—and should always be prepared and positive. Failure to be prepared and positive can have very serious consequences, as famously happened to Gerald Ratner when he criticized his own products in a speech at what he thought was a private dinner. Although Ratner was only joking when he referred to his jewellery products as "crap," a reporter published the comments and Ratner's business virtually disappeared overnight.

The idea

The founder of a magazine for internet enthusiasts used to carry anything up to 250 back issues of the magazine in a backpack wherever he went. He thus always had a copy (or even more than one copy) to hand out to anyone who might be interested. He also wore a shirt with the company name and logo on it at all times, and talked about his product at every opportunity—to the point where friends and colleagues began to ridicule him.

Such devotion to spreading the word about his brand might seem over the top to a British audience, but, as he said himself, "If you don't love your brand, you can't expect other people to." Less extreme examples might be gym owners who talk continually about exercise and sport, flying school owners who talk about the fun of aviation, bookstore owners who discuss literature, and so forth.

In various ways, we are all able to demonstrate our interest in our own brands—and, as the man said, if you don't, who will?

In practice

- Be prepared to promote your brand at any and every opportunity.

- Be positive at all times—you never know who's listening.

- If you are not enthusiastic about your brand and business, nobody else will be: maybe you're in the wrong business!

DEVELOP ALL THE ANGLES

TRULY NEWSWORTHY STORIES are golden opportunities, and do not often appear in most firms. Yet many newsworthy events or actions are only reported in one or two places, simply because the person handling the PR has not been sufficiently active in thinking through the possibilities.

The most obvious place to send a press release may not always be the best, but by examining the possibilities from all angles the PR person can place the story in many different places.

The idea

Good PR people will consider all the possible outlets for a news story, and will send out tailored versions to each periodical. For example, a new vegetarian restaurant might write an article emphasizing the healthy qualities of the food for a fitness magazine, an article on the appearance of the food and quality of the ingredients for a restaurant critic, a story about the business model for the financial pages, and a write-up about the restaurant's female managing director for a women's magazine.

Each story derives from the basic "we're opening a new restaurant" story, but each one adds to the interest value by taking a stance that matches what each journalist is looking for. The basic story is probably unpublishable—an editor would have to be pretty desperate for something to fill up space—but the derived stories have angles that would resonate with each columnist.

In practice

- Think through all the angles.

- Check on what each journalist likes, and send them that.

- Never send out a blanket release to everybody—it just creates work as journalists try to figure out the relevance of the story.

19 CREATE A PHOTO OPPORTUNITY

THEY SAY THAT a picture is worth a thousand words. For most newspapers and magazines a striking picture can take up more space than a thousand words, and takes a great deal less effort to produce. Getting the photographers along to your media event will make the story a great deal more publishable, and will also create a great deal more interest among your publics.

For this to happen, the story must be visually exciting as well as newsworthy, of course. Finding something that will make a good news photograph is a challenge, but it is a challenge that can be met, with a little creative thinking.

The idea

A razor manufacturer that had a new type of blade to promote offered a £1,000 charity donation on behalf of bearded celebrities who were prepared to have their beards shaved off publicly. The company contacted a rock star, an MP, and a comedy actor, all of whom agreed to take part. The company set up a barber's chair in Parliament Square in Central London, and invited the press to send photographers along.

The resultant pictures were widely used, and of course the company was mentioned in many of the stories (although the blade itself wasn't). The company capitalized on the event by using its own photographs of the occasion in its advertising, so readers made the connection between the company and the stunt.

In practice

- Ensure that you have something photogenic: celebrities are always good, but other possibilities might suggest themselves.

- Don't forget to invite television news crews as well. Good photo opportunities are also good video opportunities.

- You will need to back up the story with other communications, e.g., advertising, if readers are going to make the connection.

CREATE A FEATURE

THE MEDIA, AND especially television companies, are always on the lookout for good, interesting ideas for documentaries. They need shows with strong human interest, and preferably ideas that are unusual takes on topical subjects.

Any TV show has to be of interest to as wide an audience as possible, of course: humor, human interest, tragedy, or topicality are clear factors in the interest value of a documentary. Bringing these factors to bear is not always easy. Also, TV documentary makers are not going to produce a half-hour- or hour-long plug for the company and its products, so any expectation that they will do so is doomed to disappointment.

The idea

A company specializing in recruiting Australian teachers contacted a TV company with an idea for a documentary. The documentary makers were offered the chance to follow two Australian teachers as they experienced working in Britain: the show highlighted the differences between teaching in Australia and teaching in Britain, the discipline problems in British schools, the much higher level of bureaucracy in Britain, and the difficulties the Australians experienced in fitting into life in a new country.

As a fly-on-the-wall documentary the show was a great success: it had human interest (people being placed in a difficult and challenging situation), personal interest for the audience (seeing what actually happens in schools, and how it might be different elsewhere), and elements of humor and tragedy as the Australians met with triumph and disaster. An extra advantage for the TV company was that the show could be sold for broadcast in Australia.

Of course, the recruitment company got very few mentions during the show, but any interested parties would have had little difficulty in recognizing the firm, and since the show was broadcast in Australia as well as Britain it went out to exactly the right target audiences.

In practice

- Think through the whole idea from the viewpoint of the TV company. What will they gain from it? What spinoffs might there be?

- Accept that you will get a lot of coverage, but very few direct mentions. Consider the implications of this.

- Be prepared to put a lot of time and effort in, since you will be expected to act as a general dogsbody for the production company.

WRITE A FEATURE

A LARGE AMOUNT of PR is conducted through press releases—so much so that some people think PR stands for "press release." However, it is perfectly feasible to write a much longer piece if there is something useful for you to say.

As always, a feature cannot be merely a long advertisement for your brand or company. It should be something that is of general interest to a large number of people, and you cannot merely plug your own services.

The idea

A firm of lawyers in London was looking to increase its conveyancing business, so one of the partners wrote an article on ways of cutting the cost of moving home. The article examined every aspect of moving—legal fees, estate agents' fees, removals costs, insurance, and surveying costs, and explained how to make savings in each area.

The article was published many times throughout Britain, and although the firm was not directly plugging its own services the article was always clearly identified as having been written by one of the firm's partners. Every time it appeared, the firm got more inquiries for conveyancing, even though the article was often cut or even edited heavily by the periodicals it appeared in.

Articles like this can run and run, and will always make the writer look like an expert—they also generate a feeling of trust, since the writer is clearly trusting the readers with some useful information, and perhaps cutting themselves out of a fee. Readers will think of the author as someone who is genuinely out to help them—which immediately opens the door to an open and honest relationship.

In practice

- Don't mention your firm until you're well into the article—if at all. It will only be edited out.

- Give good value in the article. If it's interesting and useful to the readers, it will be published and read.

- Include pictures if at all possible. This is especially important for magazines.

22 PIGGYBACK YOUR STORY

Much of what appears in the news is PR. Often major companies expend a great deal of money and effort to get their stories into print, and to alert the news media to what they are doing.

For the astute PR person, this can provide an opportunity to hijack the publicity and piggyback a PR campaign on the strength of it.

The idea

A large American cellphone company arranged a major PR campaign to publicize its launch of what was then the world's smallest cellphone. A chain of restaurants cashed in on this by announcing a ban on all cellphones in its establishments, on the grounds that they annoy other customers.

The press picked up both stories, and asked the cellphone company to comment on the ban: stupidly, they refused to do so, and the press therefore ran with the story of the ban without mentioning the new telephone at all. This was a PR disaster for the cellphone company, but a triumph for the restaurateurs—the lesson being twofold: first, grabbing an opportunity can often pay off beyond expectations, and, second, if you have a PR campaign you must ALWAYS be prepared to talk to the press!

In practice

- Be prepared to grab opportunities as they arise.

- Always talk to the press if they ask you to—only bad things can happen if you brush them off.

- Move fast—delay will mean the other company's story goes in first.

RUN WITH THE RUNNERS

MOST NEWS STORIES come and go within a day—what is hot news today is old hat by tomorrow. There are some exceptions, though, and these can provide excellent opportunities for companies. General elections, the Budget announcement, and annual events such as Guy Fawkes Night or Christmas can provide useful points for ongoing stories.

The idea

Or ideas, rather. One clothing company used a general election to publish a list of well-dressed (and badly dressed) MPs. This was a fun, human-interest story that offered a light-hearted look at what is a serious subject.

Every Budget, a firm of accountants in the West Country publishes a list of ten predictions, and pays £500 each for any that are not in the Chancellor's speech. Other companies organise fundraising events for Children in Need or other regular charity appeals, or piggyback on events such as the London Marathon.

Regular events provide endless opportunities for PR activities: almost any regular event can be turned to the advantage of almost any business, with a bit of creative thought.

In practice

* Ongoing stories are worth latching onto.

- Keep your story light-hearted: most running stories are serious-minded.

- Be prepared in advance—you will obviously know when the event will happen, so you can be ready in good time.

CREATE GOODWILL IN THE SEASON OF GOODWILL

CHRISTMAS IS A great time for PR. People are generally full of goodwill, and appreciate goodwill gestures by companies: tying into the season is a useful tactic on several levels. First, it creates warm, fuzzy feelings among your staff. Second, it shows that your company has a human face. Third, it makes people want to reciprocate—after all, Christmas is the time of year when we give to others as well as receive from them.

Of course, it's important not to seem obvious or tacky: it's also a good idea to do something that relates to your own company's activities rather than simply run a corporate advertisement wishing everyone a merry Christmas.

The idea

In 1955, the local department store in Colorado Springs, America, decided to have a "Santa hot line" for children to call Santa Claus. Unfortunately, due to a printing error they publicized the direct line to the Director of Operations of the Continental Air Defense (now called NORAD). This was the top-secret missile-tracking system based just outside Colorado Springs.

The director quickly found out what had happened, and instructed his staff to field the calls, suggesting that they explain that the tracking system was tracking Santa's sleigh and giving updates on Santa's current position.

This has now become an annual event. Each year NORAD shows where Santa's sleigh has got to, using satellite surveillance and "Santacams" to depict the sleigh traveling across the world. The images are accompanied by commentaries from NORAD staff, Air Force staff, and national celebrities at each stage of the journey.

Although the tracking is apparently aimed at children, the opportunity is used to explain how NORAD uses its high-technology tracking equipment to protect the Western world from attack. There are links on the website to various other pages, including job vacancies and pages for potential suppliers to NORAD.

As an annual event, tracking Santa costs relatively little and creates enormous goodwill—Christmas 2008 saw 15 million hits on the NORAD website, no small potatoes for a PR exercise.

In practice

- Do something that connects to what you do rather than just wishing everyone a happy Christmas.

- Involve your employees—this will help them to get into the Christmas spirit, too.

- Put a human face on what you do.

25 TAKE THE FIGHT TO THE ENEMY

OFTEN, PR EXERCISES are aimed at publics without being specifically directed at an "enemy." In other words, if a firm is under attack, the tendency is to counter the attack in the minds of the public without directly confronting the other organization.

Obviously there is always a risk of retaliation in kind, and much depends on the nature of the exercise—but many organizations can and do use guerrilla tactics to take the fight to the enemy. Even if you don't use this idea yourself, you need to be aware that someone might use it against you!

The idea

Friends of the Earth is a pressure group dedicated to environmental issues. It is an organization that is almost entirely driven by PR: it lobbies government and industry to reduce waste, reduce the carbon footprint, and generally behave responsibly toward the environment.

During one of its campaigns to combat the use of non-returnable plastic bottles, FOE deposited 1,500 bottles outside a Schweppes bottling plant. This blocked the company's gates, but more importantly it created a photo opportunity for the local press and TV companies. Although Schweppes are clearly not the only company who use these bottles, FOE's action certainly left them with a public relations problem—and not one that could easily be explained away with a press release or two.

Generating a high-impact event like this takes planning and coordination, but the effects are likely to be large and far-reaching.

In practice

- Always try to do something that has a visual impact.

- Ensure that the press will be there on the day.

- If you are likely to be on the receiving end of something like this, enter a dialog with your enemies first!

BUILD A CORPORATE BRAND

THE CORPORATE BRAND is the overall impression the company gives to its publics, as opposed to the individual brands given to the firm's products. Building a corporate brand gives the firm a higher profile with its customers as well as with other publics, and gives credibility in all sorts of places.

Building a corporate brand is often something that companies regard as "a nice thing to have if we could only afford it" but in fact is the signal to your customers that you are passionate about what you do, and serious about being the best in your field, not just planning to earn a crust from the business. It also signals to your employees that they are working on something special: rather than working in a quarry, they are helping to build a cathedral, for example. Finally, it signals to government and local authority people that you are a firm to be taken seriously, a big player (even if you aren't).

The idea

When Edward Stobart was a child growing up in 1960s Cumberland, he (like many other little boys) liked playing with toy lorries. When he became a man, he was able to play with big lorries—he took over the family's haulage concern (part of their agricultural supplies business) and grew it into the Eddie Stobart Ltd. freight logistics empire.

Stobart knew from the outset that he needed a strong corporate brand. There were hundreds of other companies out there, many of them much longer established, so unless he was going to compete on price (which in business is the last refuge of the incompetent) he would have to compete on credibility and integrity.

Stobart gave all his trucks women's names (his first were named after prominent female performers of the seventies such as Suzi Quatro and Dolly Parton) and insisted that his drivers be smartly dressed in collars and ties at all times. Driver training is still a major part of Stobart's success—apart from hiring nice people to start with, the company trains drivers to be courteous to other road users and (of course) to customers, and to take a pride in their vehicles.

From a customer viewpoint, taking a delivery from a Stobart driver makes a welcome change from some of the greasy oafs who turn up at the warehouse demanding a signature. All Stobart staff are expected to adopt a "can-do" attitude, finding ways to accommodate customer expectations.

Eddie Stobart is now the best-known haulage company in Britain— it even has its own fan club, and people collect models of the Stobart vehicles. No small achievement for a trucking company!

In practice

- Be prepared to spend money on building your corporate brand.

- Be different from everybody else—latch onto something the others aren't offering.

- Be passionate and committed to your brand—if you aren't, no one else will be.

MOVE TO THE THIRD
LEVEL OF SPONSORSHIP

Sponsorship is a major plank in PR. Sponsoring events and organizations generates some good publicity, shows that the company cares, and often puts the company name in front of exactly the right publics.

In most cases, companies satisfy themselves with handing over cash to worthy causes in exchange for a mention in the program or on the website. This might be termed first-level sponsorship: it is, in fact, little more than advertising by another name.

Other companies move to the second level, where they will sponsor something in exchange for something else. For example, a company might sponsor a sporting event in exchange for a box at the event, or for a reception where the participants will be available to meet corporate sponsors. The company can then offer something to its clients or even its staff. This is why the Wimbledon tennis tournament always has empty seats in the stands: they have been blocked out for corporate backers of the tournament.

The third level is to find a sponsorship partner, someone who will benefit in kind as well as in cash from the sponsorship. At this level, it can be hard to distinguish between the sponsor and the sponsored.

The idea

During the 1990s, Ford found that sales of its Lincoln brand were tapering off as people switched to BMW and Lexus. The Lincoln's traditional market had been executives and professionals looking to buy a prestigious luxury car—but Lincoln had acquired an old-fashioned image. What was worse was that the average age of a Lincoln driver was somewhere in the late fifties, so Ford estimated that most of those drivers would be retiring soon and either would be unlikely to buy another Lincoln, or would continue to drive the same car indefinitely. After all, Lincolns are built to last—for a driver in his late sixties or seventies, the likelihood is that the current car will be the last he will drive.

Attracting a younger audience was essential to the plan. Ford identified a potential partner organization, a firm that was aiming at the same young, affluent, professional audience. It was a little-known Canadian circus group called Cirque du Soleil (Circus of the Sun). Cirque du Soleil is a very unusual circus, using light and dance to enhance the performances, and they were looking to enter the American market but lacked the resources to do so. Ford set up a mini-tour of major American cities for part of the circus, as a taster for their main tour. Ford dealers in the various cities sent out invitations to potential customers in the target group, and (of course) Lincolns were on display at the circus venue. No hard sell ever took place—the cars were there, the tour was sponsored, and the mailing list was retained.

When Cirque du Soleil went on their main tour, having enjoyed the advance publicity created by the Ford sponsorship, they reciprocated by acknowledging Lincoln on their publicity. The result was (a) Cirque du Soleil is now well known throughout America and beyond, and (b) the Lincoln factory in California had to go onto 24-hour shifts to meet the demand for the cars.

In practice

* Find a partner who is aiming for the same target group as you, but with a totally different product.

- Find a partner with a need either for an exciting, profile-raising partner (Ford, in the case above) or one that is itself exciting and profile raising but lacks the necessary resources to leverage their position (Cirque du Soleil).

- Work out a scheme that both of you will benefit from, and try to create a medium- to long-term partnership.

INVOLVE YOUR STAKEHOLDERS

Your stakeholders need not just be passive recipients of your PR efforts. They can join in and be part of what's happening. In fact, the greater the involvement of stakeholders, the greater their feelings of ownership and loyalty toward you and the project.

Finding something that people can buy into is an important aspect of PR. If people can see that there is something in it for them—some gain they can obtain—this makes things a great deal easier. Getting a lot of stakeholders, all with different agendas, to pull in more or less the same direction is another challenge that PR people have to face on a regular basis.

The idea

The town of Belmont, Western Australia, is actually a dormitory suburb of Perth. Belmont is about four miles from downtown Perth, easy commuting distance: the main airport is at Belmont, and the town is located on a bend in the river (a major asset in bone-dry Western Australia). It is also near the ocean and (thanks to the airport) has the best public transport infrastructure in the region. It has a low crime rate, good local schools and shopping, and some excellent parks.

Unfortunately, though, being near the airport means that much of the town is given over to warehouses and industrial parks. Belmont had a reputation for being dull, industrial, and characterized by low house prices. The town council therefore hired a PR consultancy to revive the image of the town and attract inward investment—

something of a challenge, since even the people who lived there had a low opinion of the town.

JMG, the consultants concerned, decided to create a strong brand image for Belmont as the "City of Opportunity." The logo for this was designed to fit alongside the council's crest on the letterheads, and also on the letterheads of local businesses. Using this single brand, JMG coordinated the local businesses' marketing. A loyalty card for residents was issued, offering discounts and other benefits if they shopped locally: this not only increased business for local firms, but also helped to foster a sense of community.

Local businesses were offered free marketing consultancy, and key stakeholders (local estate agents, developers, investors, shopping centers, community groups, and government agencies) were targeted specifically to get them on board. The City of Opportunity logo appeared in the windows of businesses, on business cards, and on letterheads.

The result was an investment influx of A$150 million in the first three years of the scheme, a reversal of the population decline, and a sharp rise in house values (well ahead of anywhere else in Western Australia). Major firms such as Nestlé have established themselves in Belmont, and civic pride has returned to the town.

In practice

- Consider the agendas of the stakeholders you want to involve.

- Find the common ground—in this case, the City of Opportunity slogan.

- Consult stakeholders—don't try to dictate.

SPONSOR SOMETHING IN B2B

Most sponsorship is aimed at encouraging business-to-consumer relationships, but there is really nothing to stop business-to-business companies sponsoring appropriate events. Typically, business-to-business markets are characterized by having relatively few customers, so those you have are worth impressing.

We tend to think that business buyers are not affected by emotional considerations, so a business buyer who supports Manchester United will not increase his purchase of left-handed sproggletackets just because their manufacturer sponsors the team. This is far from being the case—industrial buyers are still human beings, and are as affected by emotional considerations as are the rest of us.

Of course, they need to justify their decisions—after all, if we as consumers decide to buy something, we don't have to justify it to the boss!

The idea

Inmarsat is a company that provides cellphone communications services to ships, aircraft, and workers in remote parts of the world. In effect, the company provides cellphone services where everybody else is out of signal, because its systems work direct to satellites without the need for a network of ground stations. Obviously, this service comes at a price, so Inmarsat deals mainly with corporations such as shipping lines, oil exploration companies, mining companies, and airlines.

Inmarsat sponsored the World Rally Championship for several years. The rally emphasizes driving in remote and inhospitable parts of the world—precisely the locations where Inmarsat can provide service—and so it matches exactly with the company's image of reliability and tenacity in the face of challenging environments.

In exchange for the sponsorship, Inmarsat got TV exposure in more than 200 countries. Each of the 14 stages of the rally provides an opportunity for corporate hospitality, and Inmarsat technology is used to relay information to the TV stations that give updates on the progress of the rally. Without this technical input, TV stations would be very limited in their ability to report progress on the rally, so of course they are happy to acknowledge the source of the information. This in itself provides a dramatic demonstration of the company's technical capabilities.

Participative sponsorship, in which the relationship goes beyond a mere exchange of money for publicity, is a growing area. Inmarsat has certainly created an impact with its innovative approach.

In practice

- Find something that demonstrates your capabilities.

- Look for the spinoffs: the corporate hospitality possibilities, the TV link-ups, the news value.

- Ensure that your B2B customers know what you're doing.

WRITE A NEWSLETTER

INTERNAL PUBLICS CAN sometimes be forgotten in the drive to create a top-class external reputation. Yet employees are extremely important—apart from the need to motivate them to work effectively, employees talk to people when they go home. They are the ambassadors of goodwill for the company: if they bad-mouth their employer, they will be believed by their families and friends.

People devote a great deal of their lives to working, and not just for money. If we were motivated just by money, we'd all be pornographers and drug dealers, because that's where the money is. As things stand, we all try to do work we find agreeable for employers who treat us with respect.

There are many ways in which employees can be brought on board: a newsletter is one of them. It provides a non-threatening communications link between management and staff, and (perhaps more importantly) among staff. It also helps to generate a feeling of belonging, which is good for morale.

The idea

Newsletters are simply a brief outline of the latest developments in the firm. They can be produced in hard copy, with or without illustrations (desktop publishing makes it easy to include photos or cartoons), or can be produced electronically. The choice depends on whether employees are all on email or not.

Employees should be encouraged to contribute their own news. Knowing that Jane in Accounts is expecting a baby, or that Eric is moving house this weekend, may seem irrelevant to the management but it helps to create a sense of community. In larger firms, staff might be encouraged to tell the newsletter when they have pulled off a successful deal or had a breakthrough in developing a new product. This can be an important source of information for senior management, since it indicates what people are most proud of in their work.

News from management should be about things the staff will be interested in, such as a big new order, a successful new product launch, or somebody getting a promotion. Negative news should be avoided.

In practice

- Publish regularly—once a week or at least once a month.

- Don't let the newsletter become a propaganda device for management.

- Encourage staff to contribute. At first the contributions will be poor—let them get used to having a newsletter, and the quality will improve.

- Only include positives in the newsletter. There are other places to discuss negatives.

TAKE CONTROL OF YOUR INTERVIEWS

JOURNALISTS EXIST TO write news stories. They do not exist to promote your company. This is so obvious it shouldn't need stating, yet many people manage to allow journalists to take control of the interview, and in so doing enable the journalist to create a story out of it by quoting out of context, by directing the interviewee to say something he or she had not intended to reveal, or even by misrepresenting the person's statements.

In fact, the vast majority of journalists are fair-minded and try to give an honest account of the story, but at the end of the day they are under pressure to write the news—and that can sometimes get in the way of fair reporting.

The idea

This idea is from a publisher of a computer magazine—someone who really knows how to deal with journalists!

You need to ensure that the journalist is getting down what you say accurately, so the first question is "Are you recording this, or should I speak slowly so you can take notes of everything?" The best outcome is if the journalist is making a recording, so remember to speak clearly anyway for the tape. Alternatively, have the interview conducted via email. If it is to be done this way, reassure the journalist that you will be giving blunt, honest replies, not PR-speak. Finally, don't be drawn into saying what the reporter wants you to say. They often look for examples of conflict, and will tend to encourage you to reveal plans aimed at damaging your competition, for example.

Think about what you are going to say before the interview begins. This will save disappointment later!

In practice

- Try to ensure that the interview is being recorded in some way other than simple note-taking. This will reduce the chance of accidental or even deliberate misquoting.

- Aim to give interviews by email if possible, but don't use this as an excuse to hand out some standard, sanitized phrases. You certainly don't want to alienate the reporters by using PR-speak.

- Don't be drawn into saying something you didn't intend to say. You can't withdraw a statement once made, and speaking "off the record" is unhelpful and dangerous.

- Don't feel the need to fill a silence.

- Assume that your worst sentence in the interview will be the lead sentence in the finished story. This will focus your mind!

32 LET PEOPLE RIP OFF YOUR IDEAS

MOST FIRMS GET defensive about others piggybacking on their main brands. Some firms even go so far as to take legal action against anyone who dares to encroach on their territory—as has been the case with McDonald's, who have even tried to protect the "Mc" prefix. This was a forlorn hope in Britain, where the law allows anyone to operate a business under his or her own name, even when that name is already in use by someone else—with so many Scots having names beginning with "Mc" (and a fair number being called McDonald), there was no chance whatsoever of the courts upholding any such action. McDonald's just managed to make themselves look foolish and oppressive.

Contrast this with Toys "R" Us, who have never taken any action against firms such as Tiles "R" Us. Toys "R" Us know that the other firms will actually help promote the Toys "R" Us brand in a light-hearted way.

The idea

Weblogs Inc. is a company that makes weblogs commercial. It was founded in 2003, and hosts around 150 weblogs. The profit comes from advertising revenue—weblogs attract very specific audiences, and advertisers find that they have a high success rate when they advertise on a Weblogs Inc. site.

From the very beginning, Weblogs Inc. has taken a laid-back attitude to other people using the format and even the brand name. For example, a Spanish entrepreneur set up Weblogs SL to operate in the Spanish-speaking world, without permission from the American company (although he does acknowledge the American source for the idea).

The founders of the company say, correctly, that the imitators will only ever be imitators. They cannot catch up: all they are doing is making Weblogs Inc. look good to its publics by implying that it is worth imitating their business plan and brand name. As the founders say, one yacht crossing an ocean looks lost and adrift: 40 yachts look like a race.

People who adapt your brand name push you further up the ladder: those who steal your ideas completely look like thieves, and will not command respect. Suing them just makes you look bad.

Clearly the founders got it right, since Weblogs Inc. was sold to AOL in 2005 for a reputed $25 million.

In practice

- Don't sue small companies that are stealing your ideas. You will just look like a bully.

- Be positive about firms that copy you. It only makes you look better.

- Remember that thieves are unlikely to be trusted by customers—you have little to fear from this type of competition.

JOIN A TRADE ORGANIZATION

ROTARY CLUBS, CHAMBERS of commerce, and the like have a long history. They provide networking opportunities for businesspeople, and can often be a source of new business. Local and regional business opportunities abound, but developing a good relationship with other local businesses is a worthy aim in itself.

Many such organizations themselves need PR assistance, but rarely have anyone professional to help out.

The idea

After joining the organization, volunteer to become its press officer. This will put you in the driving seat: you will be the first to hear about new developments, you will make yourself popular with other members, and you will establish more and better contacts with journalists.

Being a press officer for the organization itself does not mean, of course, handling PR for the members. They will have to fend for themselves. What it does mean is contributing something tangible at a fairly low cost in time and effort, and simultaneously widening the reputation of your firm and yourself.

Don't worry too much if you aren't very experienced in PR. Nobody else will be either, unless they have someone experienced already— in which case the job will not be available (although it could be extremely productive to volunteer as deputy, since you will have the opportunity to pick up a lot of tips).

In practice

- Join a suitably effective organization—ensure the people you should be associating with are also members.

- Volunteer for things. If you put yourself about, only good things will happen.

- Be proactive in asking for roles, producing articles, and dealing with the press.

34 ░ TELL THE WHOLE STORY

OFTEN FIRMS WILL issue a press release about an exciting new product, but, unless there is really something very interesting about the product, the journals will simply spike the story.

Stories about new products are almost always going to look like thinly disguised advertisements. Newspapers do not exist to publish free advertising—they charge for space—but they will publish something interesting.

The idea

When James Dyson launched his new upright vacuum cleaner, he simply did not have the resources to run the kind of advertising campaign the product warranted. The cleaner's innovative design made it stand out in the showrooms, but it cost around double the price of a conventional vacuum cleaner and the advantages were certainly not immediately obvious. Dyson decided to engage the potential customers by hanging a tag on each machine that explained the difficulties he had encountered in designing the vacuum cleaner and getting it onto the market.

The tags were an immediate success. People enjoyed reading the Dyson story, so Dyson went one step further and gave interviews to selected reporters (rather than issue a press release). The thrust of the stories was Dyson's life experiences rather than the features and benefits of the vacuum cleaner, but the stories and the tags enabled potential consumers to become involved with the whole Dyson story: people's natural tendency to admire the lone inventor, struggling to get his ideas to market, helped develop a lot of goodwill toward Dyson.

Telling the whole story made Dyson a success, where other lone inventors (Sir Clive Sinclair is one) failed to catch the imagination of their markets.

In practice

- Tell the whole story—hold nothing back.

- This idea works best if there is a human interest element to the story of your new product.

- Back up the story with some point-of-sale reminders.

- Engage your audience.

WRITE A LETTER

LETTERS COLUMNS OF newspapers often offer an easy way to get your story across. Of course, you have to have a good letter to write, and preferably one that is newsworthy in itself.

Writing an open letter to a business rival can be a very effective ploy, especially if the rival has said unkind things about you—this is your chance to reply in public!

The idea

Sir Richard Branson is one of the world's great self-publicists. He has a talent for promoting himself and his companies in controversial and exciting ways, none more so than his various airlines. When he launched Virgin Blue in Australia, the boss of rival airline Qantas, Bob Dixon, made a number of statements to the effect that Virgin Blue would never succeed. Three years later he made a further comment to the effect that Virgin Atlantic would never be allowed to land in Australia, at which point Branson put pen to paper.

In an open letter sent to newspapers throughout the world, Branson repeated back some of Dixon's statements about Virgin Blue, and showed how they had been proved wrong: he then went on to offer a wager. He said that if Virgin Atlantic were not allowed to fly into Australia within 18 months, he would personally wear a Qantas stewardess's uniform and work on Qantas' London to Sydney flight, serving their customers throughout. If, on the other hand, Virgin were allowed in, he would expect Dixon to don a Virgin uniform and work the Virgin flight. Branson attached a mock-up picture of a Virgin stewardess with Dixon's head superimposed.

Dixon turned down the offer, saying "We are running an airline, not a circus."

The result of this letter was, of course, widespread publicity: Branson came out looking like a confident, clever entrepreneur, while Dixon came out looking like a humorless curmudgeon. In the event, Virgin Atlantic was given landing rights in Australia, so Dixon would have lost the bet—but, in any case, Branson came out the winner.

In practice

- Be sure to have your facts right. Don't make any statements that might be construed as libellous.

- Be humorous rather than nasty: nobody respects someone who bad-mouths their opponents, but people are generally fairly positive about jokes.

- Make sure your opponent has plenty of opportunity to reply: the response will generate as much publicity as the original letter.

GET YOURSELF ON THE EXPERT COMMENTATOR LIST

TV AND PRINTED news journalists often need to find an expert who can talk on a given topic. I have a friend who is (he thinks) the only Welsh-speaking astronomer in Wales, so he is always getting called by the Welsh-language TV and radio stations to make a comment about almost anything scientific.

Reporters simply don't have time to start looking for somebody if there is a breaking news story. They need to consult a list, find someone who should be able to say a few words, and contact them within minutes of the story breaking: otherwise they can be scooped by another medium or (worse) might say something stupid because they have not been able to consult an expert.

The idea

Contact your local TV station, radio station, or newspaper and tell them about yourself. It helps if you have an area of expertise that is likely to be newsworthy—for example, if you are an airline pilot, fire safety expert, or finance expert—but obviously your expertise must link to your business, otherwise there will be little or no PR value for you.

You may not be called upon very often, but, when you are, your company name will almost certainly be used (since it explains why you are a credible spokesperson) and your status will be enhanced considerably.

A further plus is that you will usually be paid an appearance fee—nothing big, but almost always worth while. The PR value to you in the eyes of your staff, customers, and financiers is obviously very large indeed—as long as you don't say anything too silly, of course!

In practice

- Be prepared to drop everything to speak at a few moments' notice.

- Get the journalists to brief you beforehand—it may give you a few moments to gather your thoughts.

- Be honest—if you don't know the answer to a question, don't lie about it, just say what you do know.

- Don't try to plug your business. You will get a mention anyway, and if you push it you won't be asked back.

37 GIVE A SPEECH

Throughout the country there are organizations such as Rotary Clubs, Chambers of Commerce, Women's Institutes, and even universities where guest speakers are welcome. Trade organizations such as the Chartered Institute of Marketing hold regional events every month at which a guest speaker is invited to present. All of these speech-giving occasions are an opportunity for the speakers to plug their companies by presenting as the expert.

The idea

Contact your local organizations and offer to give a speech. You will probably need to make it accessible for a general audience, and you will certainly need to make it lively and fun.

Most such organizations will be looking for a speech from an expert, on a topic of interest to the membership: you should not try too hard to plug your business, but you will obviously be using anecdotes from your own experience. Structuring the speech is straightforward: begin by telling them what you are going to tell them (i.e., explain what the topic is), then tell them (give them the main content of your speech), then tell them what you just told them (sum up and conclude).

If you aren't used to speaking for an audience, remember that the most effortless-looking speeches are usually the ones that have involved the most preparation beforehand—you need to go over and over what you want to say until you are fully confident. Don't stand stock-still reading from notes, do use marker pens to draw on flip charts or dry-wipe boards, don't use PowerPoint unless you really have no choice—audiences find it extremely boring nowadays. Talk to your audience in the same way you would talk to an individual— crack a few jokes, ask a few questions.

There are plenty of books around to advise you on public speaking, but mostly it comes down to relaxing and just talking about what you know!

In practice

- Prepare well beforehand, and keep it interesting—avoid PowerPoint!

- Provide plenty of opportunity for questions. If the group is small, allow questions as you go along.

- Try not to stick too rigidly to a pre-written script—it's boring.

- Take plenty of business cards and sales information.

38 ▮ THINK LOCAL

MANY FIRMS TRY to segment their markets by age, or income, or attitudes. Yet the most telling thing about someone is none of these—it is where they live. Where we choose to live says more about us than anything else, simply because we choose to live in places that we personally find conducive. People who like the countryside live in the country, people who like plenty of nightlife live downtown, people who like family life live in the suburbs, and so forth.

This is why people often develop fierce loyalty to their region, and even their neighborhood. For the astute public relations practitioner, this represents a golden opportunity.

The idea

Tesco, Britain's biggest supermarket chain, has run a Computers for Schools exercise every year since 1992. For every £10 a customer spends in store, Tesco gives the customer a voucher that can be collected by local schools and used to buy computers.

This is more than just a sales promotion, though. Note that the vouchers do not benefit the customer directly: they benefit local schools. The Tesco customer has the warm feeling of helping a good local cause, but without actually having to spend anything. Tesco has the kudos of helping a local cause, while still operating on a national basis—yet the cause is branded across the country rather than being linked to a specific area. The scheme not only has an effect on the customers, but also creates a degree of gratitude among the children who benefit from the computers—and children grow up to be grocery shoppers.

Finally, Tesco has ensured that a higher proportion of school leavers are computer-literate and therefore are likely to be useful employees— many of the children who benefited from the original 1992 scheme are now adults working for Tesco.

In practice

- Find something that taps into people's sense of community.

- Only run the scheme at times when it will create most benefit. Don't run it all year round, or it becomes part of the furniture and fades in people's consciousness.

- Let your customers pass on the goodwill. They will feel better for it, and think better of you, too.

39   S**T HAPPENS

SOMETIMES NEGATIVE NEWS stories break, giving the poor old PR person a nasty surprise. In many cases, company PR people try to suppress the story, or issue counter-stories to deny what has happened: this approach might work in some cases, but in most it will simply spur journalists on to find more negative stuff, if only to justify their initial story.

What companies should do, and often don't do, is accept that bad things happen and go with the flow.

The idea

Managing public relations for pop groups is always risky, as PR consultancy Henry's House found out when they were managing PR for S Club 7. During 2000, the story broke that the band had been using soft drugs, and one tabloid ran a front-page headline "Spliff Club 7."

The consultancy quickly realized that they had no chance whatever of stopping the story, so they simply contacted the journalists and cooperated with them to ensure that they got the facts right and presented a fair picture of the events. The agency reasoned that the story was going to run anyway, but by being honest and upfront with the journalists they maintained open communication and built goodwill for the future.

As always, bad news is soon wrapping fish—unless you take an obstructive or devious attitude with the press, in which case they will simply keep digging.

In practice

- Be prepared to come clean with the press.

- Don't always try to counteract a story—if it's too big to stop, you have to cooperate with the inevitable.

- Maintain good relationships with the journalists—it will pay off in the long run.

STIMULATE DEBATE

PRESSURE GROUPS ARE great for creating negative stories about products and companies, and no pressure groups are more adept at this than the environmentalists. The environmental lobby sees itself as campaigning for a crucial issue—the saving of the only planet on which humanity lives—and in view of the importance of the issue one can hardly blame them for being extremely determined in their approach.

This does, of course, leave firms with a lot of firefighting to do, and many of them immediately become adversarial in their behavior. Direct attacks on the environmentalists are unlikely to do anything other than fan the flames—but entering into an honest debate might well be more successful.

The idea

During the 1980s, research by the British Antarctic Survey revealed that there was a massive hole in the ozone layer, centered over the Antarctic. The ozone layer is what protects us from excessive ultraviolet light and damaging cosmic rays, so it is of considerable importance. The British Antarctic Survey research indicated that the hole was caused by the use of CFCs (a gas) as a propellant for aerosol sprays.

The British Aerosol Manufacturers' Association wanted at first to produce press releases showing how important aerosols are to business and consumers. This was intended to counteract the negative publicity generated by the environmentalists. However, the BAMA's PR consultants, Grayling PR, realized that telling people how convenient it is to have aerosol hairspray would be unlikely to carry much weight against the Doomsday scenario coming out of the Antarctic.

Grayling advised highlighting exactly what the industry was doing, and would do in future, to remove CFCs from their products. Grayling were able to point out that the BAMA had set a deadline for removal of CFCs well ahead of the international deadline, and invited debate from the environmental lobby to help meet the requirements even sooner. By showing that the industry was reacting responsibly to the issue, the BAMA took the sting out of the argument and allowed its positive messages to get through.

In practice

- Meet issues head-on: don't try to skirt around them.

- If the issue being presented by your opponents is more important than anything you can bring to bear, you have no chance of fighting it.

- If you are under attack from someone more powerful than you, you have to show that you are responding to their claims.

41 BE CHEEKY

MOST PR IS conducted in a fairly gentlemanly way, as indeed is most business. Now and then, though, someone will pull a really cheeky stunt—and often there is PR value attached to it.

Some of the cheekiest stunts have taken place in the airline industry. The low-cost airline business is, by its nature, fairly cut-throat. Margins can be very tight, and the industry relies on the aircraft flying full pretty much all the time—there is very little margin for error, and not much respect for competition.

In this environment, even a small change in circumstances can be enough to bankrupt an airline: irreparable damage can even be done by a small error in programming the computer that makes the bookings and therefore automatically sets the prices.

The idea

When new low-cost airline Go opened its doors for business, it represented something of a threat for established airline easyJet. easyJet rose to the occasion, though—they booked ten seats on Go's inaugural flight, and filled the seats with easyJet employees dressed in company uniform. The easyJet staff spent the flight handing out leaflets to the other passengers, promoting easyJet.

Obviously this is a stunt that could have gone dramatically wrong— Go customers might well have felt that easyJet weren't playing by the rules, and of course the Go cabin crew might have prevented them from handing out the leaflets. Ground staff might have realized what was going on, and prevented them from boarding in the first place. In fact, anything that Go might have done to scotch the stunt would have been likely to have backfired, since (for example) refusing boarding to passengers who have paid their fare simply because of what they are wearing would have made a great news story in itself.

In the event, the cheeky stunt made the news, and easyJet's reputation as a fun, enthusiastic airline was enhanced.

In practice

- Always make sure that any stunt links firmly to the news.

- Make sure you have your own photographers on-site, even if the news and/or TV people have said that they will be there.

- Remember that any stunt is a gamble—cheeky ones like this even more so. They can backfire.

WRITE A CASE STUDY

IN THE BUSINESS-to-business environment, and even in many consumer industries, there are times when simply talking about yourself becomes tedious for the readers. If you're in consultancy, training, education, or anything where you are helping clients, you could gain a lot by talking about your clients rather than yourself.

Companies such as trainers and consultants often have trouble establishing credibility with new customers. After all, you are expecting people to commit to you before they know whether you're any good—and that takes a great deal of faith.

The idea

What many firms do is write case studies about their clients. Obviously the clients have to be happy for this to happen, and you won't be able to put anything in there that is confidential, but in many cases the clients themselves are more than happy to have some extra PR at no cost or effort to themselves apart from approving the copy.

The case studies can go on your website, or if they are newsworthy enough they could even be sent to trade magazines. A good case study need only be a couple of hundred words long, but it's a triple-win situation. You get publicity and improve your own credibility, your client gets extra coverage with third-party endorsement from you, and the journals get good, interesting copy that fills a space. Another plus is that case studies have a long life—they are less time-sensitive than news stories.

Almost any consumer service industry can produce case studies. A flying school could run profiles of successful students, talking about their background and reasons for learning to fly: a hair salon could produce a write-up about a client who has appeared on TV or been voted Woman of the Year, and so forth.

As always, the key is to be alert for opportunities.

In practice

- Always check with your customer before using them as a case study.

- Give as much detail as you can—if you can quote figures for improved business, for example, then do so (even if you only say "Our client's turnover increased 23 percent in a single year").

- Use the human factor as much as you can. Quotes from your contact at the client firm will always go down well: pictures are even better.

RUN A SURVEY

NEWS MEDIA EXIST to disseminate facts, and also to entertain their readers and viewers. While it is often difficult to access news media (especially television) with a straight news story, it can be relatively easy to do so with an entertaining piece.

Newspapers and TV news often run stories about amusing surveys that have been conducted, and surveys have the advantage of appearing factual (even if they have not been conducted very scientifically). In many cases, a survey does provide genuinely useful information, of course.

The idea

Nescafé is Britain's best-selling coffee brand. For many years, the company ran a series of advertisements centered on a burgeoning love affair between two neighbors who join each other for a coffee, in different circumstances. The romantic and indeed sexual connotations of sharing a coffee have become well established in the culture.

In Britain, as in many other countries, inviting someone in for a coffee after a night out often has other connotations—it may just be an invitation to finish off the evening with a friendly coffee, or it may be an invitation of a more intimate nature. Nescafé ran a survey that asked people whether they thought the line "Do you want to come in for a coffee?" after a date was an offer of a refreshing cup of coffee, or whether it was actually an invitation to move the relationship on to the next stage. The results were amusing, and the topic itself was of course one that many people found relevant:

it is certainly a situation that almost all single people encounter on a regular basis.

The survey was widely quoted on TV news, and also sparked a number of magazine articles—all good PR for Nescafé.

In practice

- Run the survey as conscientiously as possible. If you can, get a market research agency to run it for you—this will give it much greater credibility. The agency may give you a cheap price, since they will also gain PR value from the exercise.

- Choose something that will resonate with a lot of people, even if your product has a limited market. Otherwise the news media will not be interested.

- Be controversial if possible. This is true for all stories, of course, but surveys can be tedious otherwise.

INVOLVE THE EMPLOYEES

A LOT OF PR coverage is directed internally. Employees are, after all, one of the publics that a good PR exercise should be seeking to influence, and they certainly should not be ignored. Good staff relations are basic to efficient working practices—but it isn't always easy to develop an effective, friendly, sociable culture within the firm.

All too often senior management only communicates with staff when it wants something from them, forgetting that staff actually do not have the same agendas as management: for staff, work is about paying the mortgage, having social interactions, and performing interesting and useful tasks within a team. Management frequently focuses so much on the bottom line that it loses sight of the staff's needs.

The idea

Carphone Warehouse has, like many other companies, established an in-house magazine for its employees. The magazine, *In The Know*, is kept fresh and relevant by committing time and expenditure: the emphasis is very much on articles and features that will appeal to CPW staff rather than on messages from senior management.

In The Know (or *ITK*, as it is more popularly known) always features an employee on the cover. The content has information from senior management, but also has regular columns such as Out and About, which reports on company social events, and The Dating Game, in which employees are invited to suggest who should go on a date with whom within the company. CPW has a predominantly young and single workforce, so this is a particularly interesting and relevant feature for them. Employees can ask to borrow a camera to record company nights out for *ITK*, becoming "spies for the night."

In Job Centre, *ITK* reports on people who have been promoted, giving case studies about how they have achieved success. There are also cover mounts and giveaways, and regional stories from Britain and Europe.

The magazine was launched (in its present form) by CPW's PR company, GCI London, following consultations with CPW staff. CPW has a very strong corporate culture and such good employee relations that the company has won awards including *Retail Week*'s Employer of the Year award. Not surprisingly, the practical result of this is that staff turnover is extremely low, recruitment is easy and cheap, and employees are motivated by a team spirit.

In practice

- Find out what employees really want from an in-house magazine. If they don't read it, it's a waste of time.

- Focus on the staff, not on the management's propaganda.

- Involve the employees at every opportunity—don't stop at having an "employee of the month" column.

DEVELOP YOUR NEWS SENSITIVITY

NEWS HAPPENS ALL the time, and many PR firms concentrate on creating it rather than on latching onto it. However, there are only so many news stories that can come from a firm—and really very few that are all that riveting for the average audience.

On the other hand, though, there may be many news stories out there that have a bearing on your industry and on which you could comment for the news.

The idea

Amnesty International made good use of the 1999 visit of Jiang Zemin to Britain. Obviously the news media were eager to report the visit, so a week before the arrival of the Chinese President, Amnesty issued a press release detailing China's human rights violations and offering to provide a spokesperson during the visit. This moved human rights onto the news agenda, and also provided the press with a more newsworthy scenario—simply showing the President meeting the Prime Minister or the Queen is one thing, but having a controversy and, more importantly, having a few pointed questions to ask him was invaluable.

During the visit Amnesty's head of press, Richard Bunting, appeared on Channel 5 News, BBC's *Newsnight*, and a live in-studio debate about human rights in China. During the President's visit, protesters appeared wherever he made a public appearance: the Metropolitan Police's efforts to protect him from embarrassing encounters backfired in PR terms because it created even more possibilities for TV news crews to collect dramatic footage of the apparent suppression of peaceful protest in Britain.

In practice

- Monitor the news for any upcoming story that might have resonance for you.

- Prepare beforehand—in particular, flag up the issue to the press.

- Controversy is good. It can only help your situation.

LINK YOUR PR AND YOUR ADVERTISING

OF COURSE! ALL firms link their PR and their advertising, surely? Not to mention their other communications—sales promotions, personal selling, websites, etc., etc., etc.

However, most firms only make these links in a superficial way, perhaps using the advertising to refer to a particularly successful PR campaign, or creating a PR campaign based around a particular advertisement. Really slick companies will create an integrated campaign based on a combination of communication techniques, each one boosting the other.

The idea

When Sega introduced its Mega-CD games console, the company knew that it had a promotional mountain to climb. The target audience for the product was the marketing-savvy, worldly-wise, cynical, seen-it-all-before teenage market. To reach these people, Sega would have to do something seriously spectacular—so it ran a combined ad and PR campaign designed to intrigue the audience.

First, the company ran ads for fictitious products (a cat food billed as "Good enough to eat!" showing the cat's owner eating the cat food, and a washing powder called Ecco). The spoof ads ran for some weeks, but would then be "hijacked" by "pirate" TV transmitters promoting the Sega product. Billboard ads were subjected to the same treatment—the corners would apparently be torn off to reveal the Sega ad beneath.

The piracy theme of the ads appealed to the anarchic tendencies of teenagers, but more importantly the spoof caught the imagination of the media and sparked a flurry of editorial coverage commenting on the cleverness of the campaign.

In practice

- Think through your connection between the advertising and the PR elements.

- Beware that the media may not like being spoofed—ensure that they are in on the joke.

- Make sure that your audience gets the joke: sometimes people take things seriously, and then feel silly afterward.

47 BRING YOUR ENEMIES INSIDE THE TENT

THERE IS AN old saying that it is better to have your enemies inside the tent p***ing out than outside the tent p***ing in. Any large company, and most smaller companies, develop enemies one way or another—dissatisfied customers, disgruntled pressure groups, unpaid creditors, revenge-seeking ex-employees, and honest people who have an honest grievance.

In some cases, one or several of these people will set up a website dedicated to vilifying the company. Such websites are called McNitemares after the McDonald's shadow website, and although they operate on a relatively low level they can still be extremely damaging to companies.

The idea

Royal Dutch Shell is an Anglo-Dutch oil company—in fact it is one of the Big 7 companies in the oil business. As such, it has major involvement in the exploitation of North Sea oil and has many offshore facilities in the North Sea for this purpose.

One such was the Brent Spar storage facility. In 1991, Brent Spar had reached the end of its useful life, and was in fact slightly damaged (during installation), so it was doubtful whether it could realistically be salvaged. Shell conducted a scientific study that showed that the least risky way of disposing of Brent Spar, both from an environmental viewpoint and for the safety of workers, was to tow it to deep water in the Atlantic and sink it, using explosives.

Greenpeace disagreed. They occupied the rig for several weeks, and when they were evacuated they held a press conference in Aberdeen: as is often the case, the protest groups have slicker PR than do the companies they protest against. Over the ensuing weeks, Shell petrol stations and offices were boycotted or even attacked, and Shell staff were sometimes abused.

Shell eventually backed down and had the rig dismantled. Their PR people then looked for ways to prevent any such action taking place in future—and the result was the TellShell website.

TellShell is a site that offers an open forum for discussion of anything related to Shell, its activities, its employees, and so forth. The site is moderated by Shell to remove anything libellous or simply malicious, but the intention is to promote genuine debate. The running costs are relatively low, and the effect is powerful in terms of flagging up problems before they get out of hand. It also provides Shell with a source of free advice for avoiding further PR disasters.

In practice

- Ensure that the site is well publicized on your main website and elsewhere.

- Be genuinely open and honest on the site—otherwise someone will soon set up a credible rival site.

- Moderate the site to ensure that it doesn't simply become a ranting-shop.

- Get your senior people to visit the site occasionally, both to comment and to be aware of the issues.

GO WHERE PEOPLE WILL SEE YOU

PEOPLE OFTEN FEEL that they are bombarded with messages from companies. This is not strictly true, of course—bombardment is rather a strong term for what actually happens, and of course we are surrounded by messages from family, friends, the boss, and Uncle Tom Cobley and all—we simply ignore most of them.

Among the hardest audiences to reach are young people. Often they are suspicious of the older generation, who after all represent the authority that the young people are finally finding themselves out from under. Even in the 1960s we had the slogan "Don't trust anyone over 35," and most of us didn't trust anyone over 25!

The idea

During the 1997 general election, Labour realized that one of the main planks in their campaign would be getting younger voters out. Young people tend to vote for left-wing parties, when they vote at all—many do not bother to vote, and care little about politicians and their policies.

Labour's PR people decided to take the fight to the pubs and clubs where young people congregate. They put signs up in the toilets of pubs and clubs with the slogan "Now Wash Your Hands of the Tories." This humorous and unexpected approach resonated with young people in an environment where they might be expected to talk to other young people about the message—and, of course, Labour won the election.

In practice

- Find out where your target audience can be found.

- Choose a message that links to the environment in which your target audience is found.

- Do something unusual!

49 BE BOLD IN A CRISIS

CRISES HAPPEN WITH monotonous regularity, whatever business you're in. Obviously some industries have more newsworthy crises than others—a burst oil pipeline is more likely to hit the headlines than a failure in the ticket machines at a provincial railway station—but crises still need to be handled well, and a failure of the ticket machines on the London Underground would certainly make the headlines.

In some cases, companies need to be bold in their responses. There is no point in tickling a problem with a feather when you should be beating it with a stick.

The idea

Johnson & Johnson is a multinational healthcare company. Apart from producing baby powder, lotion, and the like, the company manufactures over-the-counter pharmaceuticals such as Tylenol, a painkiller widely used worldwide.

In 1982, seven Tylenol customers died of cyanide poisoning. The cause turned out to be deliberate sabotage, by person or persons unknown: in other words, some crackpot decided to poison people. Johnson & Johnson immediately recalled the entire stock of Tylenol then on the shelves of American stores (31 million bottles in all) for a total cost of around $100 million.

The FBI thought that this action was unnecessary, since all the cases had occurred in the Chicago area only, but the FBI are not PR experts. Johnson & Johnson's bold action was a PR triumph:

although sales dropped dramatically at first, within a year they had reached their former levels and Tylenol is now the biggest-selling analgesic in America.

In this case, bold action showed that the company cares about its customers: even though there was almost no chance of anyone from outside the Chicago area being poisoned, Johnson & Johnson's action reassured people and, equally importantly, it was newsworthy. At a local level, seeing company officials removing product from shelves made the news and was highly visible for the "man in the street."

In practice

- Consider the situation from the customers' viewpoint. Their confidence needs to be restored, or sales will never recover.

- No one will buy the potentially damaged stock anyway. You lose nothing by recalling it.

- Be equally bold in publicizing what you are doing. That is, after all, the point.

CATCH YOUR CELEBRITY EARLY

CELEBRITY ENDORSEMENT CAN be a major boost to PR activities, but at the same time it can be expensive—someone famous is likely to want to cash in as quickly as possible, because today's celebrity is tomorrow's has-been.

Celebrity endorsement also carries risks of another kind: the celebrity might do something disreputable (cheat on their partner, take drugs, etc.) and this might tarnish the product or company image.

The idea

Cole & Mason manufacture various kitchen products, but they are probably best known for their pepper and salt mills. These are upmarket, state-of-the-art utensils (inasmuch as a pepper mill can be) and Cole & Mason wanted to promote them effectively on a small budget.

Food shows are perennially popular on TV, partly because they are relatively cheap to make, partly because the viewers like to see good food presented well, and partly because they are effective programs for selling advertising to supermarkets. Cole & Mason decided to recruit a celebrity chef to promote their products.

The clever part was that they didn't recruit someone who was already famous: they identified a newcomer to the celebrity chef scene, and signed him up while he was still relatively unknown. They got him to use the mills on the show, and to pose for photo shoots with the mills: the photos were sent to magazines with covering stories and, where appropriate, recipes.

Lunches hosted by the chef for journalists, cooking demonstrations at exhibitions, master classes run by the chef for competition winners, and a series of postcards featuring him and his quotes about the benefits of Cole & Mason mills all followed on in a two-year campaign. In effect, the celebrity chef was the glue that held together the components of a big campaign, but it was all done relatively cheaply by signing up the chef early in his career.

In practice

- Be a talent spotter—you need to be fairly sure that your chosen celebrity will rise in fame.

- Have a bulletproof contract. As your celebrity becomes more famous, he or she will get other offers, and may very well be tempted.

- Have a wide-ranging program of events for your celebrity to be involved in.

- Try to ensure a long tail—keep the rights to all the photos, endorsements, quotes, recipes, etc.

51 LOOK FORWARD

Sometimes sending press releases out seems like a real hit-and-miss affair. Editors may or may not use the story, it may or may not be used "as is," it may or may not be read by the target audience, it may or may not go in the right part of the periodical.

In business-to-business markets this can be an even greater problem: apart from any other considerations, the number of customers you're dealing with is likely to be a great deal smaller than would be the case in consumer markets, and the same is true of the number of available periodicals.

Business-to-business companies therefore need an extra trick up their sleeves.

The idea

Most B2B journals know fairly well in advance what topics they will be covering in future issues. They will typically plan six to 12 months ahead for special features on aspects of the industry: the purpose of this is to enable the advertising salespeople to plug ads to potential interested parties. For example, a construction industry magazine might have a special feature on road building, and thus be targeting tarmac suppliers as advertisers.

Astute PR people will find out what the forward features list contains and offer to provide relevant articles and pictures for it. This virtually guarantees inclusion on the right date, in the right place, and for the right readership.

In practice

- Find out the features list as far in advance as possible, and put a marker down to supply an article and photographs.

- Plan other activities around the appearance of your article—for example, mail your customers and potential customers.

- Submit your article in good time. It is less likely to be cut that way.

FIND A FREELANCER

NOWADAYS, MAGAZINES AND newspapers are like any other business—they need to cut their overheads. Employing people is expensive, what with saving up for their holidays, paying their National Insurance, putting money aside for their old age, paying sick leave, and so forth.

The answer for many periodicals is to use freelance journalists. This is often a win–win situation: a freelancer will often be able to charge higher fees and earn more money than would be the case if he or she were directly employed, but equally the on-costs for the employer are lower, especially since the periodical can simply whistle up a freelancer if there is a shortage of stories without having to pay his or her salary in times when there isn't much work on.

This opens up an interesting possibility for the astute PR person.

The idea

Cultivate some freelancers. A typical freelance journalist will be filing material to a wide range of publications, but will in fact be a specialist on a specific topic—for example, a science correspondent might be sending articles to several national newspapers as well as radio and TV stations. This means that one press release or story might be recycled many times.

Freelancers also need to sell their work if they are to earn money, so they try harder. Not to mention that all they have to sell is their time—anything that saves them time will be welcome, and a well-written press release will save time even if it has to be rewritten to suit different publications.

Finding a freelancer is usually straightforward, because they often market themselves in their bylines—in other words, a freelancer will end the article by saying "Joe Soap is a freelance business writer" or something similar, since this may result in being offered work by another periodical.

In practice

- Keep in touch with your freelancer as you would with a directly employed journalist.

- Don't waste their time: time is all they have to sell—it's a precious commodity.

- Help them to access any contacts you may have with editors (and anybody else who might be useful)—this could be of enormous benefit to them, and they won't forget.

53 GET YOUR NETIQUETTE RIGHT

THE INTERNET IS a great source of information—some say too great—and journalists have not been slow to get involved. Researching a story used to mean wearing out shoe leather and telephones getting interviews and comments from company officers. Nowadays, there is little need to go out in the cold, since most information can be gleaned from corporate websites: journalists can be safe in assuming that companies will not complain about the accuracy of the information, either.

In the absence of good information on a company website, journalists may have to look further afield, using sites such as Wikipedia to provide information, or even going to "McNitemares" or "suck sites" that have been set up by disgruntled customers or former employees. In these cases, the information will have to be verified and the company concerned given a chance to respond—but this will put the company on the back foot.

The idea

Set up a special section on your website for journalists. You can put all your latest press releases on there, as well as being proactive in sending them out to periodicals: this will help fill in any gaps in your distribution, and also provides an archive for journalists. You can include your corporate history, the CVs of your top management, case studies from satisfied customers, in fact everything a journalist might need to construct a story.

Provide as much corporate information as possible on your website—and don't be afraid to provide a "warts and all" picture, because the internet means that people will find that stuff anyway. Better that it comes from you than from your enemies.

You should also provide contact details for anyone relevant to the press release or story—don't just refer everybody to the press office. This will enable interested reporters to verify facts and fill in any gaps in the story.

In practice

- Ensure your "press room" or "press page" is easy to find on your site.

- Provide links to other sites that may be relevant—your trade association, for example.

- Provide contact details for as many of your people as you can, but make sure they are willing (and able) to handle cold calls from journalists.

54 WATCH YOUR BACK

PR CAN WORK both ways—for you and against you. Often your enemies will be on your case, and in the electronic age they can do it very quickly and easily, online.

In this chaotic climate, it is more important than ever to keep a close eye on the internet: enemy websites need to be monitored continually, and counteraction taken when things get out of hand. Inevitably, there will always be some attacks, and in some cases they will be so unfair that you will come up smelling of roses—most people have a sense of fair play, and certainly anybody with direct experience of dealing with you is likely to be sympathetic. Of course, some firms have been creative in dealing with enemy websites.

The idea

Constant and consistent monitoring of organizations that could affect your business is a no-brainer. Countering their attacks or even anticipating them is equally sensible—but it is possible to go a stage further.

One large firm went the distance by buying out a "suck site" that was attacking it, and paying the former owner a salary to run the site as a consumer feedback site. No restrictions were put on the former owner—he was welcome to run the site in any way he wanted—but by purchasing the site the firm had much more information in a much more timely way than would otherwise have been the case. Also, the guy running the website now felt a certain obligation not to be too vitriolic, nor to allow comments that were overly damaging.

In practice

- This idea works best for large firms, but there is nothing to stop a smaller company from doing it.

- Do not try to restrict the person running the site for you. This would seem too much like bribery, and, human nature being what it is, you will only cause more problems. The person running the site will normally moderate the excesses anyway.

- Use the feedback you get wisely. Be prepared to conciliate genuine mistakes, and be prepared to admit that failures happen sometimes—we only have human beings to work with, not angels!

GO AGAINST THE FLOW

DURING THE DOT.COM boom there were many companies starting up on the internet, and most of them trumpeted their cutting-edge technology. Most of their customers found this a little hard to follow: the "look at our amazing technology" opening line was usually followed by an over-excited delivery of a string of technical jargon, incomprehensible to anybody but a committed computer nerd.

Creating an exciting PR campaign was the aim of these firms, but all they succeeded in doing was dazzling the potential customers and investors.

The idea

Sourceree Solutions was founded in 2000, and is a supplier of solutions for supply-chain event management. In other words, the company helps firms locate supplies and confirm their origin online.

Sourceree needed to make an impact both with potential clients and with potential investors (the firm was hoping for an injection of venture capital at the time). When the company started out, there were already many others offering online solutions for all kinds of problems, and in most cases promoting their wonderfully clever software. Sourceree decided to be different—after all, supply-chain solutions is a fairly mundane business to be in, and trying to make it exciting was probably never going to work.

The company's PR campaign emphasized their experience of the supply-chain event management market, and their knowledge of how a large number of businesses were now using the internet to solve supply-chain problems in ways that would have been impossible only a few years earlier. The campaign also highlighted instances where research showed the level of losses being incurred by companies whose supply-chain management was inefficient.

The campaign worked out fine. People appreciated the focus on customer problems rather than on the "look how clever we are" boasting of other dot.coms, and venture capital flowed in. The company has gone from strength to strength ever since.

In practice

- Focus on what interests and benefits customers, not on banging on about how clever you are.

- Be different—you can't stand out unless you are unusual.

- If you're in a boring business, it doesn't always hurt to admit that in your PR!

56 ❢ DO SOMETHING VERY, VERY PECULIAR

IN ORDER TO stand out, you have to be different. Sometimes this means doing something that seems absolutely crazy—and might actually BE crazy. On the other hand, it doesn't pay to look foolish. It's a fine line between being startling and being stupid.

In recent years the fast-food industry has undergone marked changes. Competition has increased dramatically, with American fast-food restaurants covering the world and British home-grown versions losing ground. People have become a great deal more sophisticated in their eating habits, too—the chips-with-everything tradition of British cooking has taken a downturn as people have become more attuned to healthy eating and more exposed to good-quality world cuisine. Rising standards of living and better home cooking have also led to the downfall of many British catering institutions such as roadside transport cafés and fish-and-chip shops.

The idea

Little Chef is an icon of roadside eating for British motorists. Established for 50 years, the chain has served up literally millions of meals, mainly traditional British fast-food mainstays such as all-day breakfasts and pie and chips.

In 2007, though, the company went into receivership, victim of falling customer demand and increased competition from chains such as McDonald's and Burger King. The restaurants were seen as old-fashioned, unhealthy greasy-spoon cafés. Chief executive Ian Pegler decided to pull off a PR coup by recruiting world-renowned chef Heston Blumenthal to revamp the menus.

Blumenthal runs what is often called the world's best restaurant, and quite clearly is neither acquainted with, nor has much sympathy for, the greasy fry-up approach to cooking. He has no real qualifications for turning around a restaurant like Little Chef (although he did eventually come up with some excellent ideas, after one or two false starts). His value lay in the PR effect of employing him in the first place—in fact, Channel 4 made a documentary about the whole process, generating considerable publicity in the national press.

Pegler could have chosen from several other celebrity chefs with better track records in turning restaurants around (Jamie Oliver and Gordon Ramsay are two obvious examples), but choosing Blumenthal was a better PR coup precisely BECAUSE he was a square peg in a round hole.

In practice

- Doing something peculiar always has more news value than doing the obvious.

- Whatever you do must work out in the end, or you will look ridiculous. Blumenthal did, eventually, manage to create some excellent new dishes for Little Chef.

- What you do must be backed up by news coverage: make sure the appropriate media are involved from the start.

57 PUT IN SOME STYLE

Many companies and brands come to be seen as staid: being boring is not always a bad thing, but for a brand that has been exciting in the past, it is not a good place to be. Moving a brand or a company to a different place in people's minds is often essential, but requires some effort to overcome the inertia of most people's thinking.

Reviving an established product is a problem that faces most firms at one time or another. Doing so is a balancing act between creating a new concept for the product on the one hand, and the risk of alienating loyal customers on the other.

The idea

The Vespa scooter, manufactured by Italian company Piaggio, has been around since 1946. Vespa is actually Italian for wasp, a reference to the buzzing noise the scooter makes: it has an iconic status deriving from the 1950s and 1960s, when it was a stylish alternative to the motorcycle.

In more recent years, though, its popularity suffered a decline, so Piaggio decided to revive the brand. Piaggio's British PR agency invited British celebrities to design their "dream Vespa," the designs to be created in reality by a vehicle customizing company. Bridget Jones author Helen Fielding designed one with accessories for the modern woman, for example, while photographer David Bailey designed a fur-covered version.

At the same time, a parallel competition was run for the general public: the winner would have their design displayed at Sotheby's, and would be given their own customized version of a Vespa ET2 scooter.

The winning design was used for publicity purposes by Vespa before being handed over to the lucky winner, but the celebrity designs were auctioned in aid of the charity Action on Addiction. The company even found a scooter customized by Salvador Dalí in 1962, and borrowed it from the Guggenheim Museum for the campaign.

The campaign as a whole generated a very large number of media permutations—it involved celebrities, a public competition, a charitable element, and even a High Street store element (Vespas were exhibited in the windows of Top Shop as part of the competition publicity). Overall, the campaign generated over 60 million opportunities to see, based on print media readership alone.

In practice

- Make sure you get a lot of entries for your competition: publicize it widely, or better still involve the media directly by offering prizes to their readers.

- Involve a charity. Celebrities are more likely to take part if there is a charitable element, but their main reason for doing this kind of thing is to increase their own exposure.

- Look after your celebrities. They get asked to do a lot of charity gigs, so they deserve to be put in a nice hotel, taken out for a good dinner, etc.

- Provide plenty of photo opportunities.

BRING IN THE SCIENTISTS

McVitie's is the leading British biscuit manufacturer, producing a wide range of sweet and savory biscuits. The company has, for some years, run an annual "Dunking Day" as a way of promoting the biscuits via the well-known habit many people have of dipping their biscuits into hot tea or coffee (dunking). The intention behind Dunking Day was to encourage tea and coffee drinkers to accompany each cup with a biscuit.

The problem was that Dunking Day had become a fairly run-of-the-mill event with little news value. Once was humorous, twice was mildly interesting, three times was pretty meaningless: the event was relegated to "special interest day" one-liners.

The idea

McVitie's PR consultants realized that they needed a story that Britain (and, as it turned out, the world) would want to hear. The consultants put forward the idea that McVitie's should commission academic research into the science of dunking, so the company engaged Dr. Len Fisher of Bristol University to investigate the physics of dunking biscuits into hot drinks.

It turned out that dunking releases the flavor of the biscuits. Photos of Dr. Fisher and his team experimenting with the biscuits were released to TV and the press, and a scientific report was produced. The result was remarkable—the story was picked up internationally, and whatever it did for Dr. Fisher's scientific reputation, it certainly put McVitie's Dunking Day back on the news map.

In practice

- Commissioning research from universities is not cheap, but it certainly has news value.

- Make it fun—the success of the McVitie's research came from the juxtaposition of heavyweight scientific research and the lightweight subject of dunking biscuits.

- Take plenty of pictures and videos of the research being conducted.

- Ensure that the scientists you use will look good on TV and can handle such an appearance: most university scientists are used to speaking to lecture rooms full of students, so this is unlikely to be a big problem.

DO SOMETHING INCONGRUOUS

DOING THE UNUSUAL is the essence of good, eye-catching PR. Doing something incongruous takes things a step further—the juxtaposition of wildly differing images is what is striking here.

The idea

The Lowry at Salford Quays, Greater Manchester, is a major arts complex. It houses the Lowry Gallery, two theaters, bars, restaurants, and several smaller art galleries, but it tends to be perceived as being solely concerned with the work of artist L. S. Lowry.

For the PR consultants involved, publicizing the complex presented numerous problems. Although it was named after Salford's most famous artist, the message needed to get across that it was a center for the performing arts as well as for paintings and sculpture: in addition, the brand itself was unknown. The PR people needed to communicate the Lowry's significance as a performing arts venue for the whole Northwest, and also needed to encourage people to buy tickets well ahead of the official opening date.

Spin Media, the PR consultancy involved, staged a "Ballerina on a Building Site" event in which ballerinas in leotards and hard hats danced on the construction site itself. This proved to be an irresistible photo opportunity for the press and TV. An opera singer sang from *The Barber of Seville* while shaving comedian Johnny Vegas's chest hair, and DJ Mark Radcliffe reported on the progress of the building during radio interviews, thus involving a younger audience.

Over the three days following the event, the box office received over 1,000 phone calls. In the first two weeks it accepted bookings for almost £20,000 worth of tickets, and the mailing list grew by 1,000 people a week.

In practice

- Something incongruous should also be something relevant to what you are trying to publicize.

- The incongruity should be visual if at all possible—you are looking for striking pictures.

- As with all stunts, you need to prepare well beforehand, and prime your journalists.

MOVE FROM THE GENERAL TO THE PARTICULAR

COMPANIES, AND MARKETERS in particular, are prone to lumping people together in categories. Marketers are great at talking about "the consumer" as if it is one person, finance people talk about "the shareholders" or "the creditors," and (crucially) HR people talk about "the staff." Obviously we need to do this much of the time, if only because it makes conversation easier, but it pays to remember that each of these people thinks of themselves as an individual.

Sometimes it is possible to emphasize this in PR, even though most PR operates through mass media.

The idea

BUPA (the British United Provident Association) is Britain's leading provider of private medical care. Founded in 1947, just ahead of the introduction of the National Health Service, it remains a vital part of Britain's healthcare infrastructure, filling in gaps in NHS provision.

BUPA wanted to improve its internal culture by creating greater employee involvement in the brand. The aim was to improve service levels and reduce customer complaints, as well as provide employees with a feeling of belonging and team spirit.

BUPA's PR people came up with the concept of "One Life." This was built on the power of one, the concept that a single person can change things. Staff with unusual talents or hobbies were invited to audition to take part in the program of events, and a video was commissioned showing interviews with customers explaining how their experience of dealing with BUPA staff had changed their lives for the better.

This approach moves well beyond the "employee of the month" award (which is often nothing more than a huge embarrassment to the recipient anyway). It celebrates individuality, and expands people out from being considered simply in their role in the organization.

In practice

- Find interesting individuals within your workforce, and celebrate them.

- Give everyone a chance to demonstrate their own individuality.

- Involve customers in talking about the contribution of individual employees.

MOBILIZE YOUR FORCES

SOMETIMES YOU WILL have to deal with a single, crucial issue by mobilizing a large number of people from among your publics. Dealing with a political issue or a local government department can seem a daunting task—it seems that all the power is on their side, but in fact that is not the case.

Local and national government is affected by public opinion: after all, council officials are answerable to councilors, who are in turn elected by the local population. If local people apply pressure to councilors, the pressure will be passed on to the local officials, often with immediate consequences.

The idea

Vodafone is one of Britain's major providers of cellphone services. The company is based in Newbury, Berkshire, a rural town surrounded by open countryside. In common with other companies in the rapidly growing cellphone business, Vodafone has grown extremely rapidly, and was at one time spread across 51 buildings within a four-mile radius.

Obviously the company needed to consolidate operations into one site, but the only site available in the area was amid the green fields of Berkshire, so the company knew they would be up against strong opposition from environmentalists when they applied for planning permission.

The targets for Vodafone's PR campaign were local politicians such as councilors and the MP, but also Vodafone employees. Vodafone were aware that having 3,000 employees meant that they had a powerful lobby—almost all the employees were voters within the constituencies represented by the politicians, and therefore would have a great deal of influence if they could be mobilized on the side of the company.

Vodafone responded directly to every protester, especially those who chose to protest through the local newspapers' letters pages: every interview request was accepted by senior management, and a brochure was produced directly appealing for support from local people in Newbury. A stand was booked at the Newbury Show, and a detailed model of the proposed development was exhibited.

Almost a year and a half after the campaign began, planning officers recommended rejection of the application. By this time, Vodafone employees were firmly onside, and 1,500 of them staged a march through Newbury in favor of the company's plan. Seven thousand local supporters of the plan were mobilized to present their views to the local council, by means of pre-addressed envelopes supplied by Vodafone. Finally, one local newspaper was persuaded to run a call-in, in which nine out of ten calls were in support of Vodafone's plan.

The final result was that Vodafone was granted permission for its new headquarters, and thus remained in Newbury.

In practice

- Decide who you need to influence, and who will do the influencing most effectively.

- Mobilize everyone who might be able to bring pressure to bear by ensuring that they get what they want from the exercise as well.

- Remember that politics is a numbers game—the more voters you have on your side, the more likely you are to win.

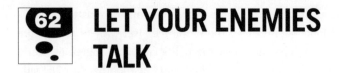

LET YOUR ENEMIES TALK

BEING ATTACKED IS not pleasant—most of us feel resentful, especially when we feel we are being wrongly accused. So a typical response from a company under attack is to try to silence the opposition—perhaps by taking out a lawsuit (as McDonald's has been known to do) or by denying access to the media (perhaps by threatening to withdraw advertising).

Although this type of behavior is very human, it is also very counterproductive—there are simply too many ways in which a protester can make his or her voice heard. The internet, the gutter press, even satirical magazines all offer access for someone to bad-mouth you.

The idea

Many major companies have "save" reps who are paid to handle complaints. The "save" reps are trained to allow irate customers to vent their anger—shouting at the rep is tolerated, up to a point, because the reps know that the customer is angry with the situation, rather than the company (and certainly not with the rep). Once the customer has ranted for a while, he or she usually calms down and a reasonable dialog can be conducted.

Translating this idea into the wider context, allowing your enemies to rant in public only gives them the opportunity to make themselves look foolish. Someone who loses their temper is likely to say things that are ill-advised: often they will overstate the case and look ridiculous to the observer, and meanwhile you can compose your response.

A good rule is to avoid being intimidated by a silence. Many people feel that they have to say something once the other person has stopped speaking—but if you wait a few moments, they will often go on to say something entirely ridiculous. This tactic also gives you time to think of a good response.

In practice

- Allow your enemy to state their case in full.

- Don't get emotional yourself—this is just business!

- Remember that the person who loses their temper is usually the one who loses a lot more.

- Don't be tempted to retaliate by suppressing your enemies—you will invariably come across as a bully, and people will assume that you have something to hide.

63 TEXT YOUR CUSTOMERS

IF THE NINETEENTH century was the age of industrialization, and the twentieth century was the age of technology, the twenty-first century bids fair to become the age of communication. We all communicate much more easily, over greater distances, and with many more available channels than ever before—and nowhere has this revolution been more evident than with cellphone technology.

Even 40 years ago, cellphones were believed to be technically impossible, because they violated the laws of physics, yet now everyone has at least one—and they represent a powerful, yet underused, PR tool.

The idea

Short message service (SMS) technology has been available for several years now, and is widely used by young people. Texting, as it is more commonly known, offers the opportunity to send messages (albeit short ones) to very specific target groups. Unlike voice-based messages delivered to cellphones, SMS is not especially intrusive: the individual can read the message any time, and of course the medium is at least semi-permanent. Messages can be kept if they are interesting enough, for example.

The prime audience for SMS messages is likely to be interested in fast food, music, films, alcoholic drinks, magazines, books, and mating-game products, but many firms use SMS simply to keep customers informed. For example, Swansea Sport Flying (a flying school in Wales) texts students to let them know that the weather has cleared for flying. Some banks (notably First Direct) will text customers to let them know when their salary has arrived, or when their account reaches a particular level (thus avoiding the risk of exceeding an overdraft limit, or possibly alerting the customer to transfer funds to a savings account). American President Barack Obama used text messages to rally his supporters during the election campaign: it has been said that his talent for getting grass-roots supporters to vote is what won him the presidency.

The key to making this work is obtaining the customer's permission to send texts. If you don't do this, you run the risk of irritating people.

In practice

- Get permission from people to include them on the list.

- If possible, use what you know about your publics to ensure that they only get messages that are relevant to them: otherwise they will unsubscribe.

- Use texting sparingly—people can easily be switched off if they feel inundated by messages.

PHOTOGRAPH THE BENEFICIARIES, NOT THE BENEFACTORS

Many companies offer sponsorship, prizes, gifts, and so forth to charities. Local newspapers throughout the country feature pictures of smiling company officials handing over giant checks to equally delighted charity fundraisers: sometimes they are shaking hands, sometimes they are just grinning like recently escaped lunatics, but to the newspaper's readers they all look pretty much the same.

This type of photo is so standard that people just skip past it. It may be a great ego trip for the guy handing over the check, but sponsoring firms need to find something a lot more interesting if the picture is going to stand out.

The idea

Phil Douglis, director of Douglis Visual Workshops, suggests photographing the actual people who will benefit from the donation. If the sponsorship is for an old people's home, take some photos of the people living there. If it is for an animal charity, photograph the animals.

Doing this will create a great deal more human interest, and it shows the actual benefits of what you're doing. The same principle applies to photographing ceremonies—getting some pictures of award winners afterward (perhaps being congratulated by friends or family) is better than photographing them on stage getting the award.

In practice

- Don't rely solely on the press photographer. Hire your own—but make sure you hire a photojournalist, not someone who takes snapshots at weddings.

- Get written permission from the people you photograph, or you may have legal problems later.

- Try to take pictures that convey some human interest, rather than posed portraits.

- Get some inside details from the people you photograph, to use in the caption or in a story.

CONSUMER SCIENCE SELLS STORIES

TWENTY-FIRST-CENTURY people often seem to be obsessed with themselves (which is a feature they probably have in common with nineteenth-century, eighteenth-century, or even twelfth-century people).

This being the case, periodicals often like to publish research that tells us something interesting about ourselves or about others we might know—and such research can be turned to your advantage.

The idea

A very large amount of research about consumer behavior is published every year in academic journals. Most of it passes unnoticed, and indeed a lot of it is hardly worth a mention anyway, but sometimes research will come up with a really interesting snippet. If it's relevant to your business, it can lead to a story in the mainstream press.

For example, a piece of research revealed that people who wear contact lenses are four times more likely to attract a partner in a nightclub than are people who wear glasses. This was of great use to a contact lens company.

Trawling through academic journals need not take up a great deal of time—usually university libraries are happy for you to browse the journals section provided you don't borrow anything or make a nuisance of yourself to the librarians, and you usually only need to read the abstracts anyway to know if the article is any use. An hour or two is likely to produce two or three articles you could draw on.

Such research, of course, carries a great deal of credibility. You should have little trouble in establishing your bona fides with the periodicals you send the story to.

In practice

- Contact the authors of the articles and tell them what you are planning. This is a courtesy, and it may lead to further information and/or research findings being forthcoming.

- Make a note of the source of your information. The newspaper will want to know where you found the research.

- If necessary, work with the researchers to produce more useful results in the future.

66 | BE QUIRKY

BEING QUIRKY OR humorous or both is a useful way of cutting through the clutter of press releases sent to journalists every day. Even TV news broadcasts like to end with a humorous piece—and getting on TV is certainly the Holy Grail of PR.

Being quirky is not something that can be achieved to order, and it is the reason why so many PR people are paid inordinate amounts of money, but if it can be done it is certainly worth doing.

The idea

PR guru Arlo Guthrie of Consult the Guru gives an example of a quirky idea that paid off. He established National Flea Awareness Minute to promote a flea treatment. This contrasted with the plethora of Awareness Weeks that crop up continually, and played to the smallness of the subject under consideration—fleas. The story made the national news, with media coverage that would equate to hundreds of thousands of pounds of advertising.

This unusual idea was humorous at the time, but it has since been superseded by a genuine National Flea Awareness Week, fronted by celebrity Anthea Turner.

In practice

- Being quirky cannot be turned on and off like a tap.

- You may need to pay someone to think of a suitably wacky idea.

- The line between quirky and just plain ridiculous is a fine one— be careful not to cross it!

END IN -EST

INTEREST IN THE biggest, the smallest, the fastest, the slowest, and the silliest will always attract people's attention ("most" is another good word). Such stories are automatically interesting, and are almost always sure-fire winners with the media because they lend themselves to eye-catching headlines.

This preoccupation with extremes is what makes people buy *Guinness World Records*, and is also a driver for people buying newspapers. Such stories often make the TV news as well, and there have even been several TV shows dedicated to extremes of weight, height, and even silliness.

They also tend to generate lively photographs, which alone is a good reason for using them, but it isn't always obvious how to link the biggest, smallest, silliest thing to your company.

The idea

Arlo Guthrie of Consult the Guru tells the story of a competition he once ran to find Britain's Most Destructive Dog. This was to promote a treatment for dogs that destroy things, and it provoked tremendous interest among the dog-owning public, who rushed to enter their pooches in the competition.

The hands-down winner, though, was a dog that destroyed its owner's car. The resulting headline, "My Dog Ate My Ford Fiesta," had reporters on the doorstep of the "lucky" winner straightaway.

Using the word "most" or any word ending with "-est" automatically raises the stakes—but it may need to be engineered into the campaign.

In practice

- Run a survey or a competition to find your "most" or "-est."

- Ensure that you get permission from the person you want to feature, and preferably get a contract for future rights.

- Make full use of any photo opportunities.

68 CREATE SOME "HOW-TO" TIPS

PEOPLE ARE CONSTANTLY looking for expert advice, and there is no doubt that running a business makes you more knowledgeable than you were before. Sharing that knowledge (without giving away all your trade secrets) is a good way of attracting attention to yourself, but more importantly it demonstrates that you know what you are doing, and can be trusted.

Demonstrating trust is a good way of generating trust. Trusting people with some of your knowledge won't make them go elsewhere—it will tend to make them want to trust you with their business.

The idea

Write a series of "how-to" tips for the layperson. For example, if you are in the building trade, some tips on how to check your house over to make sure it will withstand winter may well generate some business—and it is exactly the kind of advice people will want to cut out and keep. Someone finding a problem has your number to hand, and can tell you exactly what they need you to do.

Likewise a hairdressing salon can give tips on looking after hair between visits, a restaurant could publish recipes, or a driving school could issue advice on safe driving. The possibilities are endless, and almost any business could benefit from this approach.

In practice

- Write tips that people can easily understand, and that are useful to the layperson.

- Don't worry that it will harm your business—people are more likely to come to you, since they will trust your knowledge.

- Make yourself available for interviews for the newspapers or even broadcast media (radio shows often bring in experts).

BAD NEWS TRAVELS FASTER THAN GOOD NEWS

MOST PR EMPHASIZES the positive. Companies write nice fluffy-bunny stories about themselves and their industries, in the hope that people will think positively about them. In most cases this is definitely the best approach: enough bad things happen in the world without calling attention to them.

However, as we all know, newspapers thrive on publishing bad news. Everyone has heard of the newspaper that carried only good news, and had to close within a week because nobody was interested.

Overcoming this apparent divergence of interest creates an interesting PR paradox.

The idea

If there is a crisis in your industry, put yourself forward as the spokesperson. Often, you can find a crisis without one being immediately obvious—for example, the credit crunch that started in 2008 affected nearly every business in the country, but few of them fielded a spokesperson to talk about how the crisis was affecting business.

The idea works best if you have a solution, or a set of suggestions, for overcoming the crisis. This will make you popular, and will also make you appear knowledgeable—an important spinoff. Another major plus is if you are in a position of some authority within your industry: a prominent member of its trade body, or an executive from one of the largest firms in the industry, or perhaps simply the winner of an industry award.

Cashing in on bad news may seem a little heartless—but if by doing so you are helping mitigate the crisis, that can't be a bad thing.

In practice

- If a crisis doesn't happen all by itself, go and look for one.

- Establish your credentials as industry spokesperson.

- If possible, involve your trade association, but be careful not to let them take over!

DEVELOP A COMPANY HISTORY

STORYTELLING IS PROBABLY the oldest form of entertainment human beings have. We all love a good story—which is why we have so many conversations, why we delight in telling each other what happened to us last week, and why we like to listen to such stories. We like history, too, which is why costume dramas are so popular on TV.

Company histories combine these elements to create something that is truly of interest.

The idea

Many large companies publish their corporate histories on their websites. H. J. Heinz, for example, has a detailed history of the company on its site, going back to the days when a young Henry Heinz grew horseradish to sell to local grocery stores. The history emphasizes Henry's personal values of thrift, honesty, and fair dealing (with the clearly stated implication that this is how the company is run to this very day).

The Heinz history is illustrated, is interactive, and is comprehensive. Not all companies would have the resources to create such a web page, but even the smallest company can make a human-interest story from their history: Lucie's Farm, a supplier of Highland beef, tell the story that their founders (Craig and Marjorie Walsh) first became interested in rearing Highland cattle after seeing the film *Rob Roy*. They are now the leading breeders of these cattle outside Scotland: the farm even has its own crest. This kind of story is a great deal more interesting than features about the quality of the beef, or the problems of rearing hairy cattle in a warmer climate than they have been used to.

In practice

- Emphasize the human aspects of your history. No one's interested in your balance sheet.

- Put your history on your website and in your printed promotional material.

- If your history is interesting enough, see if someone will make a documentary about you.

GIVE A GIFT THAT REALLY DOES SOMETHING

CORPORATE GIFT-GIVING is a well-established PR activity. Thanking your most loyal customers by giving them something nice, rewarding staff with freebies, or handing out company calendars to your most efficient suppliers is common practice in many firms.

However, as we all know, having 15 company calendars and six from the local takeaway, plus eight diaries and 23 desk sets does little for your well-being: probably most corporate gifts of this type end up in the bin. This does nothing for your reputation, and still less does it do anything for the recipients of the gifts.

The idea

Choose either a gift that is unique or one that will still be appreciated even if it is duplicated. For example, the House of Commons has Scotch whisky bottled and labeled for MPs and others to buy as gifts for colleagues, constituents, staff, and so forth. Even if someone were to receive several bottles, this would not be a problem, and having a bottle of whisky with the House of Commons crest on it is a good conversation-starter at parties or at Christmas.

Hiring a cartoonist to draw a caricature of the recipient can be a lot less expensive than you might think. One corporate party organizer arranged for a cartoonist to mingle with the guests, drawing each one: the cartoonist charged £300 for the evening, and drew more than 50 cartoons. Paying £6 a time for an original caricature is extremely reasonable, and it makes a memorable gift for anyone.

Promotional clothing can be good in the right circumstances: if you are in a business where special clothing is needed (for example, if you are a motorbike training school) you might want to consider having coveralls printed with your logo. Discreet is better than obvious, of course.

In practice

- Think about your gift: would someone be happy to get three or four of them?

- If possible, give something that is personal to the recipient: it is more likely to be kept if it is personal.

- Try to avoid the obvious, and do ensure that your gift relates to your business.

PROFILE YOURSELF IN WIKIPEDIA

PART OF THE internet revolution has been the proliferation of online information services. People research almost anything online: students use the internet to research for assignments, buyers use it to source suppliers, and authors use it to create case studies.

One very widely used site is Wikipedia. It is an online encyclopedia (for anybody who doesn't know this already) that is created by its contributors. People who know something about something can write an article for Wikipedia, but must demonstrate that they have researched the topic well and the article is factual.

Obviously this is difficult to police effectively, and no doubt a great deal of stuff appears on Wikipedia without being especially accurate, but it is still a very frequently visited site.

The idea

Wikipedia has a policy of allowing anyone to enter genuine information onto its pages. This does not mean you can insert an advertisement, but it does mean you can put your company history on the site. Note, however, that any other Wikipedia user can edit the article, and although the Wikipedia administrators are fine about people altering articles they will not tolerate malicious editing, vandalism, or outright commercialism.

Wikipedia lends itself to PR, and many firms have written their own entries. This puts the company on the map, and often results in further publicity as the company is cited in articles elsewhere.

In practice

- Be truthful. If you aren't, someone else will be!

- Accept that Wikipedia is, in effect, an open forum. You can't prevent someone else adding to your profile—some company histories on Wikipedia now contain embarrassing revelations about violations of workers' rights or breaches of codes of practice.

- Ensure that visitors to Wikipedia can obtain information from your own website as well.

73 JOIN LINKEDIN

Social networking sites have become very big business indeed, with sites such as Facebook and MySpace linking people all over the world. Apart from linking up old friends, sites such as Facebook enable people to meet new friends through mutual friends.

For businesspeople, the choices are fewer, but one site does exist to provide businesspeople with a way of networking.

The idea

LinkedIn is a networking site for business professionals. It enables people to contact former colleagues, find people who might be of mutual benefit, and provide opportunities to extend one's reputation.

LinkedIn is a way to extend your reputation by using the contacts your colleagues and business associates have. It also enables you to do your friends a favor by putting them in touch with each other—only good things can come of this. You will need to be generous with your time, of course—you should be prepared to offer help to other people on the network, because that is what networking is all about.

There is, of course, nothing to stop you using Facebook or MySpace in a similar way—in each case you can upload pictures of yourself and your business, although you do need to be careful not to be too overtly commercial when using normal social networking sites, since their rules specifically prohibit commercial exploitation of the site. However, no such restrictions apply on LinkedIn: the purpose of the site is to foster business networking.

In practice

- Be prepared to spend some time contributing to the site. In particular, be prepared to help people who contact you through the site—this is about building your reputation, not about selling your products.

- Don't be afraid to ask for help yourself. That's what the site is for.

- Try to involve all your business contacts. The wider the network, the better the results.

- Make sure your business contacts don't mind being added to the site—they will be asked anyway, but it's better coming from you.

USE TESTIMONIALS

THE BEST KIND of PR is the PR that comes from your customers (and indeed the rest of your publics). What you say about yourself is always a little suspect—people are well aware that you have a vested interest. But what your customers, staff, suppliers, and so forth say about you is far more credible.

Testimonials have, of course, been in common use since Victorian times, but the age of communications has provided us with a lot more possible ideas.

The idea

Ask members of your publics to write you a testimonial. If they don't have time to do it, write it for them and ask them to approve it—obviously you need to be fairly careful here, since people do not always like to have words put in their mouths.

Testimonials are best used on your website and in publications (such as brochures) that people ask for. Using testimonials in advertising is often regarded as suspect—this is because communications that are unsought are assumed to be biased, whereas information someone has asked for is assumed to be fairly accurate.

A good way to encourage your clients to write testimonials (at least, if you're in a business-to-business market) is to ensure that they plug their own business in the testimonial. If you're writing the testimonial for them, this is something you should do on their behalf.

In practice

- Always ask people if it's OK to publish a testimonial on their behalf.

- If people are busy, offer to write it for them—but be sure that the "too busy" statement isn't just a polite way of saying they don't want to be featured.

- Only use the testimonials in sought communications such as websites and brochures.

AUCTION SOMETHING

CHARITIES ARE ALWAYS strapped for cash, and they are always looking for publicity. This means that they are usually pretty switched-on about PR: after all, if it's for charity they have a relatively easy time of it in terms of getting air time and press space, as compared with a commercial organization.

Rattling a collecting tin on a street corner rarely works effectively—in fact, the people doing the collecting would probably raise more money by putting in some overtime at work for a couple of hours, and donating the money. So charities are usually looking for something a bit more high-profile, and a bit more lucrative.

The idea

Run an auction on behalf of a charity. You can ask people to contribute goods and services, but fairly obviously the top items should come from your business. Run the auction in an easily accessible place, and if possible get somebody famous to conduct it: this will increase the likelihood that the press will attend.

The idea works best if what you are auctioning is something high-profile and/or of high value: if you auction off a holiday in the Seychelles, this has more impact than auctioning a weekend break in a country hotel. If you have something topical to sell, so much the better: during the 2009 recession, cars were not selling at all, so auctioning a car might create a considerable impact. Your decision has to be based on how much you can afford, of course.

Involving other people in the exercise may dilute your PR value to an extent, and could result in the exercise being hijacked by someone with a more exciting contribution, but it will help to share the costs.

In practice

- Find someone high-profile to conduct the auction.

- Involve the charity's PR people as early as possible. They have a lot of useful experience.

- Make sure the publicity promoting the auction has your name on it. Choosing the right product from your range will help.

SPONSOR SOMETHING FOR YOUR CUSTOMERS

Sponsorship is a very widely used tool of PR, and there are many ways of leveraging it to your greater advantage. Yet many companies don't look beyond the obvious: having the company name on the theater program is all well and good, but it doesn't have a long-term impact once the show's over.

Getting a longer-term result from sponsorship is a perennial problem, and one that has developed many solutions. Here is one that might help.

The idea

Coding Monkeys is an award-winning website design company based in Suffolk. The company is small, but very effective at creating websites that really work—easy to navigate, well maintained, and full of relevant information.

Coding Monkeys say that they had a look at the extra mile, and it was traffic-jammed, so they go further again. One of the things they do is sponsor an animal from the World Wildlife Fund on behalf of each of their customers. This fits in with the company brand, and it provides the customer with a regular reminder of Coding Monkeys each time they receive a bulletin from "their" animal.

The cost is relatively low, and it creates some immediate goodwill with the customers as well as providing a novel bit of PR for the wider world. Obviously it isn't always possible to sponsor an animal—but there are many other long-term deals that can be found so that the client gets a regular reminder of what you've done on their behalf.

In practice

- Try to sponsor something that links to your brand, or to your client's brand.

- Choose something that can be individualized to the customer, rather than just making a charitable contribution.

- Something that will generate occasional news for the client is preferable.

PUT YOURSELF ON YOUR WEBSITE

Websites are becoming the cornerstone of good PR as people rush to them to check out companies they are planning to sell to, buy from, or work for. Most websites cater admirably to these publics, yet few of them feature the boss.

The technology exists to put video clips on the website—so what's stopping you?

The idea

Some bosses are using their websites to explain job vacancies. Having someone talk through what the job entails and what kind of person the company is looking for has a great deal more impact than a dry advert in the Situations Vacant column of the local newspaper, and brings the whole process down to a personal level—which is, of course, what business is all about.

The idea can extend to other areas of the business. You could explain what you want your suppliers to do, explain what you can do for customers, or explain your ethical stance. Videos can be changed regularly, and they don't take long to make: you could even have a guided tour of the business, or show some satisfied clients.

Having someone senior talking on the website dramatically improves the human face of the company. Too often, people talk about "faceless" corporations: yet it is so easy to add a face.

In practice

- Don't do this unless you feel confident and relaxed in front of a camera. Many CEOs have made complete idiots of themselves by starring in their own advertising.

- Don't make the clips too long. They will take too long to download, and not everybody has a state-of-the-art computer and internet connection.

- If possible, get someone professional to make the recording. Don't be tempted to get your sister's teenage son to do it with his Christmas-present video camera.

78 | CHECK OUT THE BLOGS

There are many weblogs and forums out there, some of which are dedicated to sharing experiences of dealing with local businesses. For example, TripAdvisor carries customer reviews of hotels throughout the world.

The problem for the businesses is that the comments tend to be derogatory. People are much more likely to vent their spleen on a website than they are to be complimentary, although sometimes people feel moved to be nice about somewhere. Monitoring the blogs is therefore an important PR activity—as is ensuring that people say nice things about you.

The idea

Check the blogs regularly. Most of them offer the businesses a right to reply—and you should seize the opportunity. Often you will be able to identify the person making the complaint, and can contact them to make amends—if you make this offer on the blog itself, it will go a long way toward repairing the damage.

Straight refutation of the complaint, or (worse) self-justification, can be seriously counterproductive. You need to state your case, sure, but you can be a little humble about it!

Don't be tempted to get a friend to post a glowing recommendation on the blog. They rarely read true, and the blog master will take exception to it if you are found out.

In practice

- Be prepared to admit it if things went wrong and it was your fault.

- Learn from the comments.

- Don't be afraid to contact people who complained. Only good things can come of it—and people are less likely to be vitriolic if they are dealing with a real person rather than a weblog.

PARTNER WITH A CHARITY

Many companies carry out charitable works or make charitable contributions, sponsoring this and that, but relatively few will go the step further and establish a longer-term relationship with the charity.

Becoming involved long-term can be of real benefit to businesses: apart from ongoing PR value in terms of making the company look good, there is value in shared promotions.

The idea

Find a charity (perhaps a local one) that is prepared to partner with you. You should try to find one that fits with your business, of course, but that shouldn't be too hard. In exchange for supporting the charity in terms of hosting activities, helping with fundraising, contributing time, expertise, or goods and services, you should be able to arrange for joint promotions.

This can be extremely important, since most charities have mailing lists. They won't give you the list (the Data Protection Act would preclude this) but they may well be prepared to let you send out a joint mailing, especially if you pay for the mail shot.

Forming a long-term relationship like this is bound to generate many opportunities to promote your business alongside the charity.

In practice

- Choose your charity carefully.

- Remember it's a partnership—you have to give as well as receive.

- Don't abuse the mailing list.

ENTER COMPETITIONS

80

MANY INDUSTRIES AND trade organizations have competitions for members. Whether it is the Advertising Excellence Awards, the Hairdressing Championships, or the sausage-making competition, the publicity spinoffs are incalculable for the winners.

Winning an award is not just an ego trip: customers value them, especially in service industries where they are (in effect) buying a pig in a poke.

The idea

Find out what awards are available in your industry, and make sure you win one. This is, of course, easier said than done: looking at past winners is a guide, and knowing the judges also helps since you will have a clearer idea of what they might be looking for. Entering the competition has spinoffs for your staff as well: winning an award is a great morale booster, and even preparing for it will help to hone their skills and produce spinoffs.

If there isn't a competition within your industry, you might like to establish one. An award is a cheap enough thing to give, even if there is a prize attached: you may be able to partner up with the trade association to help with that part of it. If the award is in your company's name, it will establish you immediately as an industry leader, even if you aren't the largest firm in the business, and the winners (and subsequent publicity) will always feature your name: in other words, if it's your award, you win every time.

In practice

- Find out as much as you can about the judges—their own work, the styles they have favored in previous years, and so forth.

- Let all your employees get involved. It can only improve morale and hone skills.

- Consider starting your own competition if there isn't one already.

- Whether you win or lose, publicize the fact that you took part. Runner-up is better than non-starter.

81

BECOME SUSTAINABLE

BEING PHILANTHROPIC IS one thing—doing things that also help the business is something else. Using your employees to clean up a local beauty spot is a wonderful PR exercise, because it leads to news coverage and it also motivates your staff—they feel they are working for a caring organization. However, it does virtually nothing for the longer-term benefit of the business.

Moving from a purely publicity-oriented approach to a business-oriented approach requires a certain amount of creative thought and long-term commitment—but then PR is a long-term process, as is running a business.

The idea

Microsoft give away computers to schools. This is an example of philanthropy—the schools benefit from the free computers, and Microsoft creates a feel-good factor with the parents, teachers, and children.

However, the real pay-off is that the computers (of course) are loaded with Microsoft software. The children therefore grow up with Microsoft, the teachers have to learn to use it, and even the parents are likely to use it if they have a computer at home, simply because they need their children to be able to transfer easily between home and school.

Equally, Procter & Gamble have the problem of trying to do business with people in the developing world who live on less than a dollar a day. The company therefore invests in projects that use P&G

products to create a higher level of earnings. This is very much a long-term strategy—it may be 40 years before the programs show results—but for P&G this is not a problem. In the meantime, they are still getting all the benefits of being philanthropic.

Becoming sustainable in this way adds value to your philanthropy and creates a long-term benefit for your company.

In practice

- Think long-term. What you give today may not pay dividends for years—but it will pay off eventually.

- Be philanthropic by all means, but keep an eye on the long-term sustainable benefits.

- Don't waste time, effort, and money on doing anything that doesn't connect directly to your business in the longer term.

USE TECHNOLOGY FOR CRISIS MANAGEMENT

CRISIS MANAGEMENT REQUIRES a rapid response from the PR people, but much of the focus on crisis response is directed outward, to external publics. PR is also important to internal audiences, though—customers, employees, and even shareholders.

Getting the message out quickly is obviously of prime importance, and that's where communications technology comes in.

The idea

When a mentally ill student went wild with guns at Virginia Tech in 2007, authorities were criticized for their poor response times. The gunman began by shooting students in a dorm building, then two hours later he attacked students in the main building, killing a total of 32 people before committing suicide. In the intervening two hours, students were not warned that there was a gunman on the loose, so the death toll may well have been higher than it need have been.

The college authorities had difficulty in contacting all students, and since then they have put a system in place (provided by Peer Systems) that contacts students rapidly via text messaging, email, and Facebook.

Research showed that, while some students checked their email once a day or even once a week, they would often check their Facebook pages 30 times a day. Most of the students had cellphones, and the Peer Systems software was able to send texts automatically to all students in the event of a crisis. Keeping the systems up to date meant requiring students to provide their cellphone numbers, and give permission for them to be used: for Facebook, students had to accept the college as a "friend" on their page. Obviously all students had an email address that was provided by the college, but it turned out that this was less effective than the other methods of communication.

Peer Systems sell their software to many organizations, both governmental and commercial organizations. Anybody needing to contact a lot of people quickly needs a similar system.

Setting up a communications system like this is perfectly feasible for contacting customers, employees, and others in a crisis. All you need is their cellphone numbers, email addresses, and (if possible) Facebook or MySpace addresses.

In practice

- Don't abuse the system by sending out sales pitches. If you do this, people will unsubscribe or simply delete messages.

- Remember that young people are much more likely to check Facebook than they are to check emails.

- Separate out the different groups on your database—not everyone needs to get every message.

- Make sure you have people's permission to keep and use their details, or you may fall foul of the Data Protection Act.

GET THE SEARCH ENGINES WORKING FOR YOU

According to research conducted in 2007, 98 percent of journalists go online daily: 92 percent of them are looking for specific articles, and 76 percent are trawling for news sources. Like anyone else who goes online, they will enter a few keywords into the search engine and wait for results. They will, of course, keep looking until they find someone with relevant information—so it might as well be you!

Algorithmic search engines are literal-minded. They search for words in their literal meanings, but many press releases are written in ironic or humorous styles. This means that search engines may well miss your story altogether. So how do you optimize the chances of finding your website among all the billions of others on the net?

The idea

Writing the press release or the website using the most appropriate keywords is a way of ensuring that your site comes up in the first ten on the search engine list: since few people need to look beyond the first ten, or 20 at most, this raises your chances dramatically.

This means that your material has to be extremely carefully written, taking a fine line between being boring and being findable. Knowing what the keywords and phrases are would, of course, be a big help, but luckily help is at hand.

Various companies analyze the internet to determine which are the most popular keywords and phrases used when searching for specific products or stories. Wordtracker.com is one such company, offering a comprehensive service in identifying keywords. Having obtained the keywords, all you need to do is build them into your press releases and websites.

In practice

- Most keyword agencies will give you a free trial.

- Make sure the keywords you include are relevant to the people you want to attract to your press release or website.

- Don't be tempted to include every possible keyword—your writing will suffer as a result!

84 GET YOUR OWN DOMAIN NAME

EVERYBODY USES EMAIL, in fact it's amazing that the Post Office still has anything to deliver. What many of us in small businesses do is use something such as Hotmail or Gmail for our email address, because it's cheap or free.

This gives a poor impression to customers, though: it looks as if you are not serious about your business.

The idea

Major companies have their own domain names, and there is nothing to prevent you from doing the same. Acquiring a domain name is not difficult, and it isn't expensive either: companies such as GetDotted.com will sell domain names from as little as £2.99 a year. This gives unlimited email, and a website, all in your own name.

The PR advantages are obvious. With your own domain name, you look serious about what you're doing. You are easier to find online because search engines will often go directly to your site. Your brand name or company name goes out on every email you send.

With your own domain name your staff can also have dedicated email addresses, which increases the exposure of your brand name, especially if you are in a business where a lot of emails are sent out.

In practice

- Choose a name carefully—you will have it for a long time.

- Remember that you have to keep paying for the name or you lose it.

- If necessary, buy up similar names to prevent your competitors hijacking them and redirecting inquiries to their own sites.

85 USE A LOOKALIKE

FOR SEVERAL YEARS now Britain has been in the grip of a celebrity fever. People who have made even a few appearances on TV are accorded celebrity status, and invited to appear on various "celeb" shows. Being famous for being famous is nice work if you can get it—and they usually charge plenty for appearances at PR events.

Having a celebrity at your event will of course increase its visibility and improve the photo opportunities, but at a price: even D-list celebs are pricey, and celebs have the further disadvantage of being sometimes difficult to work with—many are unreliable, demanding, or lackluster when they do appear. But what's the alternative?

The idea

Some people are born lucky. They look like someone famous. Looking like Pierce Brosnan or Jennifer Lopez might be a great thing in a nightclub or when speed-dating, but it also means that the person can make a good living appearing at PR events.

The cost is obviously a great deal less than hiring the real celeb, and the lookalike is more likely to take a professional attitude to the whole thing. Some lookalikes practice sounding like the real celeb, and all will turn up dressed appropriately.

Obviously you need to be clear that you have hired a lookalike—you can't pass them off as "the real thing" no matter how much they resemble the celeb—but lookalikes have great potential for humor, and also make a good photo opportunity.

In practice

- Create something with impact around the celeb.

- Try to choose someone who is in the news, in particular if they have some connection with your industry.

- This idea is "just for fun"—it livens up your event, it isn't the event itself.

86 BLOGS ARE YOUR FRIEND (1)

WEBLOGS, OR BLOGS, have become the communication phenomenon of the first part of the twenty-first century. People read them, post to them, argue on them, put their opinions on them, and so forth.

Blogs are generally a good way of getting your opinions into the public domain, but they can also be used for networking—and in particular can be a useful method of reaching journalists who might be hard to find by any other means.

The idea

Set up a Google Alert using the name of the journalist you think would be the most useful to your business. Every time the journalist posts to a blog, you will be told—and you can visit the blog and comment on their post. Almost certainly they will see what you wrote, since most bloggers have an alert set up to pick up responses.

You may well end up with a running dialog, or even an argument: often this will spill over into the journalist writing a story about you, your company, or your comments. If not, you at least have someone to contact when you have something important to say.

The key point when blogging is to make a real comment. Don't just say "Great post! I couldn't agree more!" You need to open a dialog. For example, "I read your post, and in my experience . . .," or "If I understand you correctly, we could go one step further and . . .," or even "A point you might have missed is . . ." This opens up the possibility of a meaningful dialog, and also makes it clear that you aren't some kind of sycophantic idiot with no ideas of your own.

In practice

- Identify your target carefully, and find out which blogs he or she visits.

- Set up a Google Alert (this is easy to do) so you know when the person has blogged.

- Make your own blog post controversial and interesting, but obviously not offensive.

87 BLOGS ARE YOUR FRIEND (2)

IF YOU HAVE your own blog, there are many possibilities for networking. The obvious one is, of course, that people visit your blog and make comments about you (positive or negative, you can use them all) and your competitors, and will also often offer possible liaisons for further business. Even if postings are negative, you have the chance to correct the situation, either by making amends or at the very least by having the chance to have your say.

However, blogs can be used as bait to catch people you want to network with.

The idea

Once you have identified the person or people you want to put yourself in contact with, mention them by name on your blog. Most journalists and many other people have a Google Alert set up keyed to their own names, so that any reference to them will result in a message to them. They do this so that they can check on any comments made about their reporting.

Therefore, if you blog about a journalist, there is a strong chance they will appear magically on your blog and comment in turn. If this miracle does not come to pass, the fallback position is to email the person concerned (subject: "I Blogged About You") and give them the link to the blog. Very few people could resist going to the blog to see what you wrote, and that's when the dialog starts.

It may take more than one try to get the person to post to your blog, but it's worth persevering—electronic communication is where it's at in the twenty-first century, and most people would rather go this route than answer the telephone or open mail.

In practice

- Wait until your own blog is well established with a number of regular contributors before you start involving your target person.

- Target carefully. Make sure the person you want is the right one.

- Write your blog so that it's interesting and thought-provoking (or rather response-provoking) without being either offensive or sycophantic: see Blogs Are Your Friend (1).

88

COME FLY WITH ME

THOSE OF US who travel internationally are familiar with in-flight magazines. These are found on most airlines in the seat pocket in front of you, and are aimed at the wealthier members of society (which is, of course, anyone who can afford to buy an airline ticket).

In-flight magazines are a neglected resource: since they don't appear on news stands and don't have a wide circulation, they don't feature in most guides to the media. That means they are below the radar for many PR people, and yet they offer many opportunities to reach a well-off, semi-captive audience.

The idea

In-flight magazines have the same need for interesting articles and news stories as any other periodical. So, for example, if you are running an event that is open to the general public, contact the editors of in-flight magazines for airlines serving your city and see if they will include you in the What's On column.

Writing articles for in-flight magazines can also generate publicity. Editors get far too many travelogues (the "what I did on my weekend away in Athens" type of story) and far too much material that is completely misdirected. An article about business trends in your country or city, especially if it is accompanied by some good photographs, might work much better. For example, an estate agent might write about property trends, a restaurateur might contribute some traditional recipes from the local cuisine, or a clothes store might contribute an article on fashion trends.

The possibilities are endless!

In practice

- As in any other magazine, you must target well.

- Remember that many people on the flight are not on holiday—they are traveling for work, and are probably not interested in your article on travel.

- Be authoritative. Only write about what you know.

- Remember that a lot of people on the flight will have English as a second or third language—keep it simple, and don't use slang or obscure idioms.

SEND A PHOTO OF YOURSELF

89

AUTHORITATIVE ARTICLES ON subjects of interest to the readership are exactly what editors are looking for. In many cases, though, such articles are dry, even tedious: an article about falling house prices and what you can do to help your home sell is interesting, but lacks a certain humanity.

Moving the article up the agenda for an editor is the name of the game, but how to inject some human interest?

The idea

Have a nice photo of yourself taken and send that in with the article. Not all editors will use it (especially if you look bad in the picture) but it will at least give them a more human angle on your story. It also helps them to see you as a fellow human being, not just another publicity seeker. It can even move your story up the agenda, from the bottom of page 16 to the middle of page 4.

If they do use your picture in your article, it makes it much more likely that people will read and remember the story. It also puts a human face on your article, and makes people more likely to respond. Finally, it makes a much more interesting clipping for your salespeople's silent sellers, or your office wall, or your brochure (be careful about copyright if you want to reprint the article, though).

In practice

- Get a good picture taken. Digital cameras have made this easy, of course.

- Update the picture regularly. Ten years ago you were ten years younger—but the photo you had taken then makes you look ten years older!

- Don't get upset if they don't use the picture. Space is often at a premium.

GRAB ONTO SOMETHING UNPOPULAR

Most PR people look for the positives, but most news is negative. At the end of 2008, the world headed into a major financial crisis (which had been preceded by a major rise in fuel costs). Most firms tried to mitigate the negatives in the news by putting out counter-stories, basically saying "The world might be going to pot, but we're still solvent."

There could, however, be a much punchier approach waiting if you grab onto the negative news.

The idea

Tell people what you're doing to combat the problem, especially if you have thought of something wild and wacky. For example, if petrol prices have risen, you might have decided to issue bicycles to your employees. If there is a credit crunch, you might run a competition for the most original idea on saving money within the firm. You might decide to make a special offer—for example, in early 2009 restaurateur Peter Ilic abandoned prices on the menus at his top London restaurant and allowed customers to pay what they thought the meal was worth. Obviously, in some cases they would pay very little, but in other cases people paid more than Ilic would have charged, and in any case he got value for money from the exercise simply because of the publicity.

Often these stories have good visual possibilities: employees riding their bikes, the lucky winner of the competition, the restaurateur serving a customer, and so forth. Equally, such ideas are valuable in their own right—putting the staff on bicycles really does save money, and Ilic reported that his restaurant was packed solid with customers. As any restaurateur knows, the key to success is filling the place up seven evenings a week and lunchtimes too.

In practice

- Watch out for disasters and get your response in early.

- Remember you can always back down later, after the story has run.

- Do something out of the ordinary—remember, other people may have the same idea.

Popular television shows offer an almost unlimited chance to pick up PR opportunities. The gradual takeover of television by reality shows and "how-to" shows provides the chance for almost any business to piggyback on a popular program.

For example, cooking shows feature recipes that rarely turn out as they should when one tries them at home: here is an opportunity for a restaurant chef to explain how the TV chefs organize themselves to create a dish. Likewise, an antiques dealer should be able to cash in on the popularity of *Antiques Roadshow*.

Good television is about people and their experiences, and so is good PR. There should be plenty of opportunities for everyone.

The idea

Keep a pen and paper handy when you're watching television. There is a strong likelihood that you will be watching programs that are relevant to the industry you're in, so it should be relatively easy to make a note of anything that strikes you as a possible piggybacking opportunity. You need to be alert so that you grab the opportunity while it is still hot, and before anyone else gets in.

You should be able to make references to most things that happen on the show, but you may need to be careful about using the names of people from it.

News programs also offer opportunities to comment—even if all you do is write to the local paper's letters column, it enables you to raise your profile a bit. Businesses are often lax about putting themselves forward in this way—but that's what PR is all about!

In practice

- Never watch TV (or read a newspaper) without a pen and paper handy.

- Act fast—these leads go cold quickly, and other people sometimes get in quickly, too.

- Be prepared to comment or offer advice on anything relevant to your industry.

92 UPSTAGE YOUR COMPETITION

Sometimes it becomes impossible to compete directly with a rival firm or event. What they are doing is just so far beyond what you can manage that you have no chance at all of attacking them head-on, so the only alternative is to make a guerrilla attack—which in PR terms means upstaging the competition.

Sir Richard Branson is a past master at doing this—turning up at opening days wearing a town crier's outfit, or making a "spoiler" announcement ahead of a competitor's grand press conference. But there is nothing to stop anyone doing it.

The idea

The DJ at one radio station realized that his show would have no chance whatsoever of competing against a major sporting event that was due to clash with it. So he said that, to show his support for the teams, on the day before the match he would sit in every seat in the stadium.

He got permission to do this, and of course the stunt made the local TV news: the shots of him moving from one seat to the next in a 50,000-seat stadium clearly made more interesting TV than yet another interview with the groundsman about the state of the pitch, or with the coaches about the state of readiness of the players.

Timing is essential—doing something on the same day cannot work, because the competitor's event will swamp it. Doing it two days before is too soon, two days after is too late: this DJ got it exactly right by acting on the day before.

Such stunts are hard work and may not always pay off—but it's better than doing nothing in the face of a juggernaut!

In practice

- Recognize when you have no choice but to use guerrilla tactics, i.e., know when direct competition has no chance of working.

- Plan ahead. You will need to think this through and prepare your response.

- Do something that links to your competitor's event, and preferably appears to support it.

THINK OF THE CHILDREN

CHILDREN ARE AN emotive issue: anyone who is, or has been, or will be a parent has at least some emotion about kids in general. Yet from a PR point of view they are often neglected, when in fact they could (and should) be a potent source of PR coverage. Newspapers and TV love stories about children, simply because they know that their readers and viewers love stories about children.

Even though children are often ignored or neglected by PR people, they have parents and grandparents, and will eventually grow up to be customers. In some cases, of course, they already are customers.

The idea

One advertising agency devised a series of tips for producing media-savvy kids. The agency gave parents a toolkit for teaching their children the difference between advertising and TV programs, and between advertising and news stories.

This somewhat unusual idea went down extremely well with parents. Many parents are afraid that their children will be manipulated by advertisers, and equally do not trust advertisers themselves: the agency helped to restore some trust in advertisers, but more importantly it showed itself to be a caring organization.

In practice, nothing is lost: children fairly quickly become media-savvy anyway, and certainly they are by the time they are making independent buying decisions, so the exercise only accelerated the process and made some parents' lives a bit easier.

There are many other ways PR stories can be generated by doing something for children: advising parents on how to prevent their children becoming overweight (this is the kind of thing a health-food store, a gym, or a restaurant could help with), or perhaps teaching kids how to look after their money (banks, financial advisers, and accountants could help here). Articles on such topics are very likely to be published by newspapers and magazines.

In practice

- Although you are doing something for the children, it needs to be something that the parents can relate to as well.

- This idea works best on a local basis, but it can be done nationally as well.

- Repeat the exercise, if it worked: it can become an annual event, because the children do grow up and others come along to replace them.

94 TELL THEM ABOUT YOURSELF

Frequently journalists will want to see a biography from you. This is so that they can fill in some gaps in what you say, and also so they can establish your credibility—do you really have the authority to say what you are saying, in other words.

Unfortunately, many people seem to confuse "biography" with CV, and send over a lot of boring stuff about which university they attended, where they have worked, and what qualifications they have.

The idea

Develop a separate biography for journalists. You can of course drop in the name of your university if you want, but if instead of saying how you graduated with a 2.1 in engineering you say that you were captain of the rowing team or you have the record for the fastest run from the lecture hall to the bar you will attract a great deal more interest.

This is because such detail makes you a three-dimensional human being, not a two-dimensional walking CV. Include items such as your interesting hobbies, your wife or husband's name and occupation—even something about your children or your pets will go down well.

One flying-school owner includes the fact that he used to fly tourists over the Victoria Falls in an ultralight. This somewhat exotic flying experience may not have a lot of relevance to taking a student up on a cross-country navigation exercise in Wiltshire, but it shows that we are dealing with an interesting person.

In practice

- Look at your existing CV. What does it say about you as a person? Not much?

- How would you describe yourself to a prospective life partner? That's the kind of stuff that makes you human!

- Tailor your biography according to the person you are sending the story to. Try to include the things that the journalist and/or the editor will think are relevant to the publication.

95 TAP INTO VALENTINE'S DAY

OR ANY OTHER romantic possibility. Given the high divorce rate, and the low propensity to marry in the first place, the singles market has changed dramatically over the last 30 to 40 years. People no longer meet up in their teens and early twenties, then marry for life: nightclubs nowadays understand that many of their customers are second-time-round retreads. Hence the over-30s nights, the over-40s nights, and even the over-50s nights that have become commonplace at most nightspots.

There is really no reason why any other business shouldn't tap into this market, though, whether it's Valentine's Day or not.

The idea

A major supermarket had the idea of running a singles night for shopping. The store opened late, but only for singles: people were able to come and get their shopping, and also meet singles of the opposite sex in a non-threatening environment. From there it was easy for people to arrange for another date, offer a lift home with the shopping, or even go out for dinner or a drink immediately after shopping.

The event was a great success, not only because it was well attended by people who spent quite a lot of money, but also because it made a great news story. Opportunities to meet potential partners are relatively fewer as one gets a bit old for clubbing, and it's easier to strike up a conversation over the canned vegetables than over drinks in a noisy bar. Supermarkets are also a more innocuous environment: plus one can see whether the other person cooks from basics, or heats up a pizza!

The idea could be extended to almost any consumer-oriented business.

In practice

- You need to be careful that people coming to the event really are single, and there are no weirdos.

- Be careful about the news media—you don't want to embarrass the customers, but you do want the publicity.

- Advance publicity is important: afterward, you can make it a regular event, even a weekly one if necessary.

PIGGYBACK ON CELEBRITY NEWS

CELEBS ARE ALWAYS in the news—that's what they do. Often, they are shown doing something silly, or something exciting, or wearing something inappropriate. Any celeb picture offers an opportunity for somebody to generate a story—especially if the celeb is doing something that relates to your business.

The key to success is keeping your antennae out, and always thinking "How can I turn this to my advantage?"

The idea

When Britney Spears was photographed driving with her eight-month-old son in the front of her car, in a forward-facing baby seat, slumped to one side, one enterprising child safety consultant generated a story about wanting to give Britney Spears lessons in child safety. This story gave people the subconscious impression that the consultant was ACTUALLY giving Britney Spears advice, which of course was not the case and was, in fact, never stated.

There are plenty of other possibilities—a celebrity who is caught drink-driving might provoke a response from a soft-drinks company or a driving school (or even a law firm). A star who appears in an ill-fitting suit might prompt a story from a tailor or a style consultant, a celeb caught "in flagrante" with a co-star might get some gratuitous advice from a hotelier or a florist.

Piggybacking on a celebrity's news value might seem a little cruel, but of course the celebrity is only too happy if the story runs and runs—after all, they are the arch-publicists, or they are nothing!

In practice

- Keep watching the news—especially the tabloids.

- Ideally, only pick up on things that have made the front page. You are producing a secondhand story, after all, which will weaken its impact.

- Be very quick—the same day if possible. If you wait a day, the original story is old news.

KEEP IT SHORT (SOMETIMES)

TYPICALLY, PR PEOPLE will tend to write lengthy pieces explaining absolutely everything about everything, and covering all the points. Most of the time this is fine—if the story has been written properly, it's easy for the editor to cut it down to size.

On the other hand, sometimes editors have a small space to fill. Editing a newspaper or magazine involves filling up a very large amount of space, and this is not always straightforward—it's often impossible to cut a large story down small enough to fit.

The idea

Most editors keep a file of "briefs." These are small stories, a hundred words or less, that can be used to fill odd spaces. Such stories are not time-specific, so editors keep them around rather as a carpenter keeps a box of nails, to be used as necessary.

Writing briefs is a different talent from writing press releases. A typical brief might consist of "five tips on . . ." or perhaps a short quiz. These are especially useful if the editor has a story on the same topic, but the story isn't quite long enough.

You may or may not be credited for providing the brief, but it never hurts to do an editor a favor—they do remember, especially if you remind them subtly later.

In practice

* Keep it, well, brief—100 to 150 words is plenty.

- Write something that is not too time-specific. The less topicality, the better chance you have of the brief appearing.

- Don't necessarily expect acknowledgment in the periodical—you will probably get a mention, but if not you may need to write it off to goodwill.

CREATE A TOP TEN LIST

TOP TEN LISTS appear everywhere—Ten Worst Dressed Men, Ten Best Dressed Women, Ten Worst Cars, and so forth. Such lists are often compiled by people who have no particular claim to be able to do so, except for being in an industry with a vested interest.

However, the news media love them. They create a human-interest story, they create debate among the readers, and they often provoke letters to the editor (another way of generating space-filling material).

The idea

Almost any business can create a top ten (or bottom ten) list. The problem is to do it without upsetting the customers, and with a degree of humor attached to it.

Compiling the list itself could simply be a matter of making a judgment yourself, or it could involve a survey or voting system: in some cases, it may be worth while to offer the opportunity for a newspaper to get involved, running the survey and collecting the votes. Understandably, they will want to share in the glory if the story gets picked up elsewhere, but it will undoubtedly guarantee publication of your list in at least one place.

Alternatively, you could have a guest list of judges drawn from your industry, or from the long list of celebrities who are prepared to judge this kind of thing—for a fee, of course.

In practice

- Choose something humorous, but relevant to your business.

- Be careful not to be libellous.

- It doesn't have to be ten—it could equally be five, or even three.

- Consider the possibility of two contrasting lists—best and worst, for example.

- This idea works best if you do it near the end of the year—the worst of 2009, for example, produced in December 2009.

DO A RANDOM ACT OF KINDNESS

MANY BUSINESSES HAVE strong associations with other businesses that are important to them. For example, estate agents and lawyers have a symbiotic relationship: lawyers rely on estate agents for conveyancing business, and estate agents rely on lawyers for referring people who are (for example) dealing with a deceased relative's house sale, or looking to value a property.

Likewise, lawyers and accountants often feed work to each other, and doctors and chemists work closely together. All businesses rely on someone else—that's the nature of business—so why not recognize the importance of these other firms by committing an act of kindness?

The idea

A law firm in Baltimore, America, knew that they relied on accountants (CPAs) for a large amount of their business. Accountants would often need to refer a client to a good commercial law firm, and of course there are a lot of lawyers out there. The law firm decided to institute a "Feed a CPA Day" on which a local catering firm would deliver a beautifully prepared and wrapped lunch to three CPAs chosen at random.

These were not necessarily firms that the lawyers dealt with on any regular basis—the point was to create a news story, not to thank anyone in particular. What it did do was put the law firm into the news story, and show that they recognized the contribution accountants make to the law business, and indeed to the world at large.

The idea can be extended to almost any business—everybody relies on some other category of supplier. Accountants are a good one, because their work receives so little recognition in the normal course of events.

In practice

- Do make sure the idea is well publicized in advance, otherwise the recipients of your largesse will be very suspicious indeed.

- Be random—giving a free lunch to your accountant is not news: giving a free lunch to a firm you don't know is news.

- Remember it's the news value you are interested in, not finding some new business associates. Don't follow up on the recipients—they will contact you if they want to (and usually they will, if only to say thank you).

100 GET ON YOUTUBE

YouTube has been the online phenomenon of the century so far. It allows people to post pretty much anything they want to on video, provided it isn't pornographic or libellous or otherwise illegal.

People like to see themselves on telly, and a huge number of people have taken advantage: everything from professionally produced clips down to cellphone videos appear on YouTube, and clips come in from all over the world.

Of course, outright commercial plugs aren't permitted, but that's not what PR is about anyway.

The idea

An artist named Valentina from California decided to expand interest in her work beyond galleries. She wanted the opportunity to explain her thinking, and show people the process of making the artworks, so she had herself filmed actually painting a new work, and giving a running commentary.

The idea took off, and she now posts a new "episode" every Sunday. Eager YouTube viewers "tune in" each week to watch her paint, and she now has a worldwide following.

Not all of these people will buy a painting, of course, but galleries have certainly picked up on what she is doing: her profile has been raised considerably. And that, as they say, is PR in action.

In practice

- YouTube will edit you out if you are overtly commercial rather than just interesting.

- Have the actual filming done as professionally as possible, but without the "Hollywood" touch. YouTube is about people, not about slick production.

- Keep it personal. Talk about yourself, not the company (although you can, of course, mention the company too).